'A cheerful, funny, compassionate collection of anecdotes about her life and her patients.' *She*

'Banter and wry social comment aerates the problems of drink, drugs and delusions. But despite her jaunty note, the perceptive, caring physician continually shows through.' *Church Times*

'The message, presented with astonishing good humour, is that you can survive hospitals – even if you're a doctor.' *Daily Mirror*

'Autobiographical sketches in a Herriot vein – it makes entertaining and pleasant reading.'
The Northern Echo

'A darlin' book by a darlin' girl.' *World Medicine*

Pass the Happy Pills

JOYCE DELANEY

SPHERE BOOKS LIMITED
30/32 Gray's Inn Road, London WC1X 8JL

First published in Great Britain by Peter Davies Limited 1978
Copyright © 1978 by Joyce Delaney
Published by Sphere Books Ltd 1980

TRADE
MARK

This book is sold subject to the condition that
it shall not, by way of trade or otherwise, be lent,
re-sold, hired out or otherwise circulated without
the publisher's prior consent in any form of
binding or cover other than that in which it is
published and without a similar condition
including this condition being imposed on the
subsequent purchaser.

Printed in Great Britain by
William Collins Sons & Co Ltd
Glasgow

To Neal Timlin, Neil Mongey and Eva Kelly, at the Bank of Ireland, Erdington, who gave me an umbrella when it was wet.

1

'Mr O'Halloran!' Sister shot back the screen shrouding the patient in the bed, who was fighting a losing battle trying to light a cigarette with a horny hand which shook from the imbibing of, according to the case-notes on my lap, forty pints of beer a day. 'If you don't put out that cigarette you'll blow us all up. There's a full cylinder of oxygen just beside you which could send us all sky high.'

'And sure wouldn't that be the solution to all our problems, wouldn't it?' Ignatius O'Halloran said with all the mordant saltiness of his Dublin origins. However, pawing at the ash-tray on his bedside cupboard he managed to squash out his cigarette and arrange the crooked spectacles on his face, which might have borne some faintly noble resemblance to a Roman Emperor except for his two rotten teeth and a slight squint.

'Well,' I said, 'I'm a psychiatrist.' 'Are you now? Well isn't that grand?' Mr O'Halloran wasn't the slightest bit put out. In fact, from the satisfaction of his tone I got the feeling that he was flattered that the O'Halloran psyche was considered worthy of exploration. Besides, although my services were all on the National Health, and although I felt that Ignatius would have preferred it if the gift had been alcoholic, he was enough of a philosopher to take whatever life served up.

The curtains parted to admit a large lady squashed into an inadequate dressing-gown, from which showed bulges of bust and belly. 'Did you see that nurse with the orange hair and the platform shoes?' she demanded. 'I've asked three times for a bed-pan and rung the bell till my finger is stiff, but nobody's come.' 'Ah, sure they'll all be at a meeting or something,' Mr O'Halloran said. 'They'll be in Sister's office talking about statistics or something. Ah, the days when a person could get a drink of water quickly in hospital, leave alone a bed-pan or enema, have gone.'

With the resignation of a latter-day 'Joxer' Daly, Mr O'Halloran replaced the screen after the irate lady had stumped off in search of bladder relief, and sighed deeply.

'They have these hostesses you know,' he went on, 'young ones showing their bottoms in mini skirts, going around asking are you all right, like air-line hostesses, but without a thing in their heads except boy friends. Oh God be with the days when you had the Battle Axe Sisters. I remember one in Jervis Street, Sister Immaculata, and by the Lord Harry, even the doctors lived in mortal terror of her. You can't beat the nuns for running a hospital. And sure hospitals these days are like hotels. I'm no prude doc, but don't you think it's awful to have men and women cooped up here together? Has modesty gone? Why should that poor woman have to ask the likes of me for a bed-pan? Is it right? Is it proper?'

Mr O'Halloran was no mean orator, in spite of the lack of alcoholic stimulation, but I had other patients to see and I wasn't going to get involved in typical Dublin chat about the absurdity of life, diverting though it was, especially as Mr O'Halloran's nasal and fruity Rathmines accent brought back happily nostalgic memories to me.

I had to get down to business. According to the case-notes Mr O'Halloran was suffering from what is crudely known as 'The Shakes', and although still not suffering from DTs, Dr Ferndale, the referring physician, wrote in his covering letter that he had no doubts that if Mr H continued to drink at his present rate, the O'Halloran liver, brain and kidneys would pack up within two years. I'd been called in to take Mr O'Halloran into Barrington Hall, the near-by psychiatric hospital, where I worked, and give him the 'drying out' treatment. I had no doubt from a lifetime's experience with alcoholics, and Dublin ones in particular, that all I'd be able to do was a sort of first-aid patching-up job. Enough to steady Mr H sufficiently to resume his daily ingestion of liquid anaesthesia.

I knew better than to leap boldly in by referring to the fact that Ignatius drank too much.

'Er . . . I believe you like a drink, Mr O'Halloran?' I began.

2

'Have you perhaps been . . . er . . . taking too much?'

O'Halloran straightened his glasses, which looked as if he'd stepped on them in his cups, and fixed me with bloodshot but bland eyes.

'I've had me quota,' he said. 'Yes, I've had me quota.' Not 'I drink too much' or 'Perhaps I've been over-indulging' – but a typical Dublin polite verbal brush-off. What *was* his 'quota'? I knew that to mention the forty pints referred to in the notes would offend Mr O'Halloran's susceptibilities so much that it would take me ages to get more information from him, so I went on to ask about his family, looking down at the list of the ten O'Halloran children ranging in ages from two years to twenty-two. Deirdre, Naomih, Orla, Ossian, Naoishe, they'd all been called after ancient Celtic Royalty.

'Oh, yes,' said Mr O'Halloran, 'I'm a keen believer in our National Heritage you know.'

I looked a bit blank because I'd never been quite sure what the term 'Our National Heritage' meant. But Mr O'Halloran had delved deeply into Irish history, he told me, and here lay his problem. Mrs O'Halloran, it appeared, didn't share his historical interests, mainly, I felt, because she was too busy dealing with pregnancy and progeny. And instead of encouraging the O'Halloran children to read books and attend to their home-work, she allowed them to watch telly, smoke cigarettes and use language which brought a blush to the hardened Ignatius's mottled cheeks.

'Oh, a good-hearted woman,' O'Halloran said with the magnanimity of the man with an uneasy conscience, 'a decent woman, but soft, far too soft and without any control over them young ones.'

I ventured to suggest that perhaps having so many children placed an intolerable burden on the over-fertile Mrs O'Halloran, and, although it wasn't my business, didn't Mr O'H think that some sort of contraceptive might help her health?

'Ah, she's not that kind,' he said. 'She's forever helping down in the parish hall and she's that addled that she got all mixed up about that Safe Period and put that thermometer thing up the wrong passage, if you'll excuse the expression. Anyway, she's

3

waiting to go in to have Everything Out.'

Mr O'Halloran regarded the cup of tea brought to him by a young nurse with extreme distaste, but he managed to sip some of it before half the contents slopped on the sheets.

If his wife was waiting for an operation then there was all the more reason for Mr O'Halloran to come into hospital and get himself fit, I said. Braving things further, because time was getting on and my bleep was whirring, indicating that somebody wanted me, I told Mr O'Halloran that, in my opinion, he'd have to give up the drink or he'd be dead shortly, and that he ought to come into Barrington Hall without delay and have a course of vitamins and sedatives.

'Of course I will. Certainly. Anything you say, Doc.'

The alacrity with which he agreed with me confirmed my certainty that I wasn't ever going to stop Mr O'Halloran from walloping back his 'quota' as soon as he could. The only thing that would stop him was when his money gave out or death claimed him. But at least I'd be giving poor Mrs O'Halloran a break by taking her husband in for a few weeks and making a badly needed bed available for St Peter's.

'I'm in your hands, Doc,' Mr O'Halloran said, looking like a crabbed cherub. I knew from experience that this was the kiss of death! Patients who said that they were in your hands usually meant exactly the opposite, and had determined that they had no intention of changing their life styles. Which in Mr O'Halloran's case meant gazing at the complexities of life through a beery dark glass.

'Thank God you're taking him,' Sister said. 'He's only inciting the other patients. And still drinking. Do you know he had the cheek to tell a probationer nurse that the contents of his bedside bottle was urine, when of course it was John Jameson whiskey brought in by one of his sons. I don't suppose you'll be able to cure him?'

What the Almighty and Blessed Mat Talbot hadn't been able to achieve was certainly beyond my capacity, I said, and went on down to see the Overdoses or ODs as they were known.

2

The Overdose brigade, as they were beginning to be known, were becoming more and more of a problem, and an unpopular one at that, in hospitals. Nurses resent having to spend precious time on people who, they feel, have made themselves ill by deliberate intent; the male doctors see the failed suicides, who are mostly women, as examples of feminine inefficiency and the women doctors get cross at members of their sex letting down the side again. What with the ready availability of pills and tablets, the lifting of legal penalties and the total lack of any stigma, it's almost as if overdosing has become the 'in' thing with the young and a subject for boasting about, as important as having done a stretch.

I saw four youngish patients who had all made abortive attempts at ending their lives by gestures varying from wrist slashing to gobbling tranquillizers, precipitated by troubles in their love life which in my youth would have been dissipated by what Wodehouse once described as a 'good blub in the lav', and I was gloomily ruminating on my function as a psychiatrist when the phone rang in the clinic room. I signalled to Sister Jolley, a portly little woman who ran the out-patients with an iron hand clothed with just the right amount of velvet to give her the necessary humanity.

'Can I see you?' It was Dr Frances Mullen's throaty voice, so I mouthed 'Five minutes' to Jolley who bustled out.

'Well, I'm just recovering from some professional overdosers,' I said. 'I can see you before I get stuck into my list.'

'I'll be right down,' she said.

Frances, or Frankie, as everyone called her, was a large woman of my own age who hailed from County Kerry. She worked in the same grade as myself at Barrington Hall and I'd known her from student days. In spite of her double chin, dew-laps and curves which had never known the confines of a corset, Frankie's luxuriant dark hair, flashing black eyes and very white skin made her look striking, to say the least of it. She would have been ravishing had it not been for the fact that everything about her was too large and her features were almost acromegalic. Typically, instead of seeking to tone herself down by wearing dark colours trimly tailored, Frankie had always adopted trailing kaftan-type garments in vividly exotic hues. She went in for bandeaux and turbans and drifting chiffon and silk scarves and once told me that she envied the way Isadora Duncan had met her death.

I took to Frankie's dramatic and rather theatrical character from the very first time I met her. In our post-war era as students, clothes were drab and utilitarian and our beaten-down confidence that resulted from the nuns' crushing influence made us creep around like apologetic mice. But not Frankie. She exuded a buoyancy and a 'take me or leave me, I don't give a God damn' air that was irresistible. I don't think she knew any more than the rest of us, but you felt, watching her stride into lectures dropping books and scarves and winking lasciviously at the lecturers, that not only had she gazed at the beaded bubbles winking at the brim of life's beaker but had a good swig at the contents as well. And in spite of her size and the fact that her nose was more than Roman, it was positively hooked, she was able to acquire an enviable legion of male admirers. One of the endearing things about her though was that some quirk in her romantic nature always made her incline to the no-gooders. Any boozer, bum or layabout appealed to Frankie as long as he could amuse her and make her laugh. For years she had had an affair with a barrister who was a hopeless alcoholic and who everyone but Frankie knew was going to end in the DTs. She fed him, bailed him out of jail and 'dried him out' until he died of some obscure disease while on holiday in the Mediterranean. After a few more ill-fated romances she married a doctor who turned out to be a drug addict, leaving her, in her forties, with no family and a load of debts.

As I sat sipping my tea I thought of the first time I'd met

Frankie. A crowd of us had gone to a dance at the boat club where as usual there were more girls than men, especially as the pubs hadn't yet shut and we females had to wait till throwing out time meant that there'd be an influx of male students rendered unselective and randy. To hide the shame of being one of the many wallflowers I went to the 'Ladies' and found the mirror blocked by Frankie, splendid in a flame-coloured ensemble. Dangling earrings shivered as she shook back her mane of hair, so thick that she could hardly drag the comb through it. After hoisting up her impressive bust with hands glittering with rings which although they might have been cheap, certainly looked impressive, she slapped on some mascara, stuck a red rose behind her ear and turning to me said, 'Christ, all I need is a crystal ball.'

I laughed and she introduced herself as Frankie Mullen. We were both second-year medical students but the reason she hadn't been at lectures recently, she said, was that she'd been off with glandular fever. I didn't like to ask but I had an idea that that was what you got from kissing!

'No use going out yet, the real talent hasn't arrived,' she said, sticking a cigarette into a long jade holder and blowing smoke with what I thought was the ultimate in sophistication.

'Joyce Delaney? I've seen you eating cream cakes in Mills's,' she said.

I had seen her too, usually surrounded by admiring men whilst I sublimated by gorging myself on as many gooey cakes as my meagre pocket-money allowed.

'The Trinity students should be here soon,' she went on. 'They're so much more civilized, aren't they? None of your open shirts and spewing Guinness.'

I agreed. We all had ambitions to get off with Trinity men who had names like Willoughby and Digby and spoke in refined Anglo-Irish accents and approximated to Oxbridge men far more than our fellow students at UCD, who to our cruel eyes seemed gauche and agricultural.

'I feel,' said Frankie, shuddering in voluptuous expectation, 'I feel like being swept off into the desert night by an intelligent Valentino. Or invited to share late supper by a genius who reads

Proust and has a good cellar. But I expect I'll end up with a yob who thinks Sixty-Nine is a Bingo call.'

I was enchanted. Her rich Kerry accent was the cream on her conversational cake. None of my friends spoke of Proust and Sixty-Nine and I could have listened to her for ever but she crushed out her cigarette and took up an enormous bag. I couldn't help seeing that there was half a fruit cake in it!

'Yes, I feel like having a night of mad passionate love-making. But what the hell can I do with Mammy bashing the bloody rosary beads at home and praying for me to retain Holy Purity?'

I was hooked. Frankie and I became great friends after that and although we lost track of each other after I went abroad and got married, I was delighted to find when I took up the job at Barrington Hall that she was also a medical assistant on the staff. She looked a bit more bloated, her face more ravaged and plenty of white streaks in that tumbling mass of dark hair, but her ebullience was undimmed and she had the triumphant air of the survivor. She had had a hard time paying off her dead husband's debts but things had now become easier, she informed me, because she had a companion with whom she shared a house.

Against all ethics she had taken up with a Major Barney Osborn, ex-Indian Medical Service, when she'd done a locum in a very salubrious private practice in the West End.

'He came to me with a sore throat,' she told me, 'and one thing led to another. He's well over sixty, no money apart from his pension and he looks like an ad for somebody's curry powder.'

It would have to be someone out of the ordinary for Frankie. She'd never gone for the ordinary nine-to-five sort of man. What about the crazy professor who'd committed suicide because of her and the tea planter who'd carried a hand grenade in his pocket when he took her out? And the maddened industrialist who'd lost her a hospital job when he'd jumped through the matron's window in mistake for hers?

But she and the major seemed to have settled down to a permanent if stormy alliance and they lived together in a drafty old house quite near Barrington Hall. There was no question of marriage, she told me, because there was a Mrs Osborn lurking in Bournemouth and anyway, she added, Barney thought more of his smelly old bulldog Willy, than any human being.

The dog was certainly ill-tempered and smelly but Frankie as usual exaggerated in her description of Barney. He was small and thin as a whippet with a choleric temperament and a maddening tendency to use his slight deafness in a selective manner but he was also amusing and lively, and in spite of the volcanic explosions of rage which both he and Frankie used to alleviate the monotony of life there seemed to be a genuine affection between them.

There was a thump at the door and Frankie swept in clad in a purple cloak and exuding an expensive waft of French scent. It was many long years since she'd had to use joss sticks. She'd been reduced to burning them to add a bit of the exoticism necessary to her nature when lack of money had forced her to live in cabbage-smelling digs.

'Listen. I can't stay. I've got hordes of mad humanity waiting to be seen. Can you come round tonight? I've got something to talk to you about.' She tried to stick a hair pin into her toppling chignon but failed and it fell on the floor. Sister Jolley had reappeared and was staring at Frankie with the half fascinated, half horrified expression which was folks' common reaction to Frankie's non-medical appearance.

'Well,' I said, 'my house is a tip and I've got letters to write. . . .'

'Those things can wait. Come about seven.' Frankie had a way of riding over obstacles.

'I'll give you a meal,' she added at the door and I must say that that did it. Amongst Frankie's accomplishments was excellent cooking and my stomach was still quavery after a tough and tasteless canteen lunch.

'I'll make a coq-au-vin.' Frankie knew my weak spots so well. 'And a soufflé. And Barney's taken to his bed so I can raid the wine.'

It was too much. I could almost taste the succulent sauce and the melting chicken, so weakly I caved in and told Frankie I'd be along after the clinic.

'Better start, doctor, some of them are beginning to complain.' Sister Jolley quite liked Frankie but couldn't disguise her disapproval of her unprofessional appearance. She'd never really get over Frankie's frequent phone calls to her butcher either. So with an 'It takes all sorts' expression in her eyes she showed Frankie out, staring at the inches of red slip dipping under Frankie's hem-line.

'Sheena Boden's your first patient, Doctor,' Jolley announced.

3

The girl who came in with her three-year-old daughter was twenty-three and with a fresh beauty that even the fashionably ragged hair style and gypsy type skirt and blouse couldn't hide. With her oval face, wide marine-coloured eyes and smooth fall of fine brown hair she reminded me of the Mona Lisa before middle age overtook her. Bright eyes, camellia skin and quick ready smile, you'd never have guessed that only a few months ago she'd been struck down by a florid attack of schizophrenia, after which it was found that she also had diabetes. Both diseases were under control now and it was most fortunate because, divorced from her husband, Sheena was struggling to bring up the child, Melinda, on her own, having no family and only Social Security to fall back on.

'How well you're looking, Sheena,' I said. 'And Melinda.' It was true. The child looked happy and well cared for.

'Yes, we're both doing fine, Melinda and me,' she said. 'But I'm terrified the schizophrenia will come back. It won't, will it Doctor? I don't remember much about it. Only how terrifying it was. Tell me it won't come back.'

She didn't remember, fortunately, but I did. It was hard to imagine that the bright, attractive-looking young girl smiling at me had been a scrawny, crazed creature haunted by delusions and hallucinations, making bizarre gestures and facial contortions as she stood cowering in a corner spitting and urinating. I could hardly belive it possible myself as I tried to blot out the memory of the distracted girl who had howled like an animal and hurled obscenities at the nurses.

I couldn't say, 'No, it won't come back.' I wanted to tell the lie but I couldn't, and anyway who could say for certain that it never would? The schizophrenia was in abeyance now and happily with the long-acting injections she was having, there was no reason why the dreadful disease should ever return. As I spoke to her I saw the fear leaving her eyes and she smiled.

'It's like diabetes, Sheena,' I said. 'We can control it with the medication you're having, the schizophrenia I mean.'

She shuddered. 'I looked it up in a book you know. Schizophrenia means splitting of the personality.'

'Well, yours seems pretty intact,' I said, writing out another appointment for her.

She got up. It was September and chilly and the thin poncho she wore seemed inadequate against the weather. But Melinda was snug in a red cat-suit. Sheena tucked a rug around her child and paused on her way to the door.

'There's something I can't get out of my mind,' she said. 'I have this feeling that I'll die in a mental hospital.'

'Don't be silly, Sheena.' I hoped my tone wasn't falsely hearty. 'You look very healthy and the way things are going, what with injections and things, there won't be any mental hospitals soon. We don't even call them mental hospitals any more. They're called "psychiatric hospitals".'

It was well after six o'clock by the time I'd finished the clinic. I'd have no time to go home and change but what the hell? That was one of the nice things about Frankie. She didn't give a damn how you turned up. Liberty Hall, that was how you'd describe Garland House, the broken-down old Victorian barracks of a place where Frankie and Barney lived.

The night was nasty and damply dark, and from the outside Garland House loomed up in all its stark ugliness. But inside Frankie had exercised all her artistry in making it bright and welcoming. She had spent a few years at art college and it showed in the colourful pictures on the walls, the profusion of trailing greenery and the comfort of the huge book-lined room into which she showed me.

'Here, get this down you while I see to the meal.' Frankie, dressed in a coral smock over black pants and with her hair hanging down her back in a thick plait, stuck an enormous glass of well-chilled white wine into my hand.

'Where's Barney?' I asked, trying to stop the smelly body of

Willy from ripping my tights.

She pointed to the room upstairs and rolled her eyes.

'Sir doesn't feel well today. That fellow's like the princess who got upset when she felt a pea under six mattresses,' she said.

There was a heart-rending groan from the room above and Frankie bellowed, 'Give me a break for God's sake. Joyce is coming up to see you.'

The groaning increased and Frankie pushed me towards the stairs. 'Go up and put chat on him. It's always the same when the weather turns a bit cold. He's convinced he's got pneumonia, although Cousins his GP was in this morning and sounded him all over. Just wants notice, that's all.'

I should have been used to Barney doing his Grand Malade act. He had elevated hypochondria to a fine art and Frankie, after years of suffering it, never seemed to be able to bring herself to ignore it because early on in their association Barney had managed to convince her that he'd got sand in his stomach after some ancient combat in the desert.

He lay back on the big double bed which was periodically used for connubial purposes looking as pink and perky as usual but the bedside table was cluttered with bottles and pill-boxes and he replaced a thermometer in a glass with a weary gesture. When I asked him how he felt he flopped back on the pile of pillows and closed his eyes. I knew he'd heard me but he was using his deafness as a defensive weapon. I sat down by the popping gas fire and my empty stomach rattled with the tantalizing whiff of coq-au-vin wafting up from the kitchen.

'How are you, Barney?' I said in a loud tone.

'Bloody awful. Bloody awful. Never slept a wink last night and had to change my pyjamas three times. Bet I've got cerebral malaria.'

'Is your temperature up?'

'What?'

'Your temperature? Is it raised?'

'I've got spots before my eyes and I can't see. That bloody fool Cousins says it isn't malaria, but he's just recovering from a cataract operation himself.'

'You look all right.' As soon as I said it I knew it was the wrong

13

thing to say because he reared up in the bed and roared.

'Never judge a book by its cover. You should know that. Christ, here I am living with a bloody doctor and nobody can do anything for me. I'm done for. Finished. And there's Frankie and she won't do me the kindness to put me out of my agony. I'd do more for Willy. Just give me a jab, one plunge and I'm gone. Nobody will know. She knows what to do. But will she? No, all she bloody does is come in and start messing around with food. What's that you're drinking?'

'Wine,' I said. His change of tone as his very bright blue eyes lingered on my glass took me by surprise.

'And doesn't anybody think that a dying man couldn't have a brandy? Or have you both become so bloody hardened to suffering that you'd let me rot here and pass out with my throat parched?'

'Oh for Christ's sake shut up.' Frankie appeared bearing a glass which she stuck into Barney's outstretched hand. 'I thought it was the undertaker you wanted, not booze. Listen, Joyce and I have had our ears blasted listening to patients all day without you doing your King Lear bit. Get this down you and shut up.'

Barney gulped down some brandy and said snappily, 'I suppose you saw-bones couldn't do your jobs without getting hardened. And you're both so aggressively healthy that of course you can't imagine what real suffering is.'

'My God!' Frankie tossed back a black plait and laughed sarcastically. 'That's good, coming from you. Hard indeed. D'you know Joyce, he badgered poor Cousins to send him to a specialist a few weeks ago. Tell Joyce what the specialist said, will you? Go on, tell her.'

Barney lay back, eyes closed and looking martyred. He patted Willy who had heaved himself pantingly beside his master.

'Tell us what Watson Davies told you, go on. . . .'

Barney gave a rattling gasp and his rosy colour darkened with fury. Frankie gave another yell at him and he snarled.

'No need to shriek like some harpie from the slums. This is the kind of indignity the deaf man is subjected to. It's why I'd rather be dead.'

14

'Watson Davies told you, in my presence, that you are as healthy as a trout and he wished he had arteries like yours,' Frankie roared triumphantly.

'What are you saying? What's she on about?' Barney looked plaintively at me though I knew he'd heard Frankie perfectly.

If I hadn't heard this sort of duet many many times I'd have thought that they hated each other and that Frankie was a hard-hearted virago with no compassion for a hard-of-hearing old man. But I knew that behind her tough exterior Frankie had a heart as soft as melted butter and that Barney, apart from his defective hearing, which wasn't nearly as bad as he made out, was indeed very healthy. But he got lonely and self-pitying and suffered torturingly jealous fantasies about Frankie, who in a weak moment, inflamed by too much gin, had told him about her ill-starred love affairs. Since then, in spite of her age and her size, he believed, according to Frankie, that every time she went out it was to some orgiastic assignment. His 'collapses' were childish attempts to gain her sympathy and attention. Although she had so often vowed to give him what she called the 'freezer treatment' and leave him alone until he came out of what were, after all, childish sulks, Frankie's tender heart always let her down and Barney's ruses won the day, just as now, when, after straightening his pillows and refilling the water jug beside his bed she told me that supper was ready and she was going to serve up.

'Oh, that's it,' sighed Barney, 'ignore the sick man. I'm a bore. I can't help it. Admit it, you're bored with me. What am I going to have to eat? Bread and water with something in it to shut me up?'

'I wish to Christ I *could* shut you up,' said Frankie. 'I thought you told me your throat was so sore you couldn't swallow?'

'It's a bit better now. No thanks to that fool Cousins though,' Barney grumped. 'I think it's the brandy that's helped. I'll have another. And I could manage a small lamb chop with a little mashed potato. And some jelly.'

'You'll manage some of the casserole we're having or nothing,' said Frankie. 'And I'll send Joyce up with a brandy. Unless you want it to arrive tied around Willy's neck.'

15

There was a flicker of a smile around Barney's mouth as he patted his snuffling dog. Really, the animal was so fat and rheumaticky that I'd often wondered how he dragged himself around. According to Frankie, Barney talked to him and even read him snippets from the newspapers.

By the time I'd got Barney his second brandy he had pushed himself up in the bed and the first drink had done its work because his eyes were twinkling electrically and he'd done one of his quick emotional changes into joviality.

'She doesn't understand, Joyce,' he said. 'Kind hearted but lacking in sensitivity. As I said, I know you doctors have to keep up a front, but as I'm always telling Frankie, don't let it develop into hardness. And of course people make no allowance for my not hearing. It's a continual agony. The deaf man is regarded as a fool and a butt for people's humour.'

He took a tremendous gulp of brandy and asked me what I thought of John Cousins? I was very careful because I knew that Frankie did illegal though lucrative locums for the GP. As far as I knew, I said, he was a good and hard-working doctor.

'Ah,' said Barney, 'but did you know his wife has some ghastly sort of creeping paralysis and there was some talk about him associating with one of the receptionists? I think he's making use of Frankie. Keeps her ages when she does a surgery for him. I don't like the bugger. Shifty. Never looks you in the eye.'

'Who doesn't? Are you on about Cousins again? Honestly, you've got a mind like a blocked drain.' Frankie came in with a loaded tray and Barney tried to pucker his face up into a suffering expression.

'Talk of paranoia,' Frankie said later over the coq-au-vin which was excellent. We were eating in a cosy wood-panelled dining-room and Frankie had raided Barney's small but select cellar for a very good claret.

'His jealousy gets worse. Try some of this soufflé. It's good.'

So it was. The Grande Marnier flavouring and the lightness of the mixture made it slip down my throat like angels' food and by the time we'd reached the stage of liqueurs I was feeling in a receptive mood so I asked Frankie what she wanted to tell me.

'It's not to tell you anything,' she said. 'It's really to ask you

.something. Jack Duggan had a massive coronary last night.'

I wasn't surprised. Duggan, the oldest consultant at Barrington Hall, had bashed his way through medicine by assertiveness and luck and for the last few years had been skating on the thinnest of medical ice. He drank and gambled too much, and since his wife had left him last year he'd become even more reckless and there had been a number of complaints from patients and staff.

'So that means there'll have to be a locum to cover his work for at least six months,' Frankie went on.

'How about you?' I said.

'Nothing doing. I do sessions for Cousins and anyway I've my hands full with His Nibs. That leaves you.'

I was flattered but flummoxed. As a medical assistant I didn't have the responsibilities of a consultant but I had almost complete clinical freedom and I liked working with Tony Manners who was the latest addition to the consultant staff.

'The thing is, if you don't take it, Munu will put in for it,' Frankie added.

That did it. Dr Munu was an enormous Nigerian who was highly intelligent but grossly paranoid and liable to stay in his rooms in a huff for days after some imaginary slight. He did his rounds in the evenings and never appeared till after mid-day. Any suggestion that he change his routine was met with a burst of anger and more than veiled threats to inform his embassy.

'You were here before Munu. He's no better qualified, so for God's sake and all our sakes, take it.'

It was all very fine I said, but what about the domiciliaries? Domiciliary visits were visits to patients' homes made by the psychiatrist at the request of the GP and Duggan did an enormous number of them, partly I suspected to help pay off his gambling debts. I didn't know the area around the hospital well, I hated driving and I'd got out of doing General Practice partly because I didn't like visiting. What on earth would I be like now, older, stiffer and without the ignorant confidence of youth?

'It's the visits. Finding the places and ... and ... facing things like dogs ...' I said.

'Oh shut up,' Frankie's brisk confidence was always able to

17

shoot down doubts. 'What about me when I did that job on the Yorkshire moors? I was stuck in a drift for a night and only for the fact that I had a slab of chocolate I wasn't found dead. And you're the one who swanned off and did a ship's doctor job? And went out to Malaya with the bandits nearly at your door step? Come on, say you'll do Duggan's locum? Or do you want Munu to have it?'

No, I didn't. So I told Frankie that I'd take the locum and she said good, she was afraid for a minute that I wouldn't.

There was a heavy thump from upstairs and Frankie ignored it.

'To think that after all I've been through I have to end up with a crotchety old bastard like Barney,' she said. 'Why do I attract the bastards? Is it some magnetic masochism that draws them to me?'

There was a crashing sound and I said ought we to go up and investigate, but Frankie said not at all, that was just Barney kicking the lavatory bowl, a habit of his when frustrated.

'Listen, I mightn't see you for a few days. Cousins is going away. That's why Barney's playing up. Because I'm going to be out and about more.'

I couldn't have managed all that Frankie did – but then Frankie was always a surprise to those who didn't know her very well and thought from her vague manner and drifting draperies that she was a bit of a Madame Arcati. In fact she was an excellent and experienced doctor and had inherited from her cattle dealer father a canny shrewdness. Of course Frankie didn't advertise the fact that old man Mullen was in the cattle trade. She thought it more romantic to say that he had been a racehorse trainer.

There was a series of lurching thuds and a stream of profanity from the landing and Barney bellowed.

'Too fucking busy lashing into my drink to bother about a poor old man. I think I'm paralysed. I've got a stroke. I'm paralysed, paralysed . . .'

'There's nothing bloody wrong with your tongue,' Frankie screamed back.

'Better go up to him.' Used as I was to the drama of their

dialogues I yielded to the quivering woe in Barney's thin shrieks.

'Oh, he's stubbed his toe or something,' Frankie said, getting up from the table. It gave me an excuse to make my departure after promising Frankie again that I'd do the locum for Duggan.

'I thought you'd see reason,' she said at the door, aiming a clout at the snuffling Willy who was lunging at my skirt as if interceding on his roaring master's behalf.

4

Barrington Hall was a big sprawling monstrosity of a hospital, and was originally built as a workhouse at the turn of the century to accommodate, among other people, lunatics (as they were then called) who at that time were dealt with by incarcerating them well out of sight of their fellows and with heavy gates, iron bars on the windows and massive railings hemming them in. Heroic efforts had been made in the last twenty years to humanize the place with bright paintwork, new buildings and the addition of many go-ahead units like Day Hospitals, an Adolescent Unit and an Addiction Centre, and social centres and shops where the patients could buy anything they required to make life more pleasant. Those of them, and they were in the majority, who were able to go out, took the bus into the nearby busy town of Rigton.

But the main part of the hospital, which was now the administrative block, retained its original Dickensian look, and no amount of decoration or alteration could change the grim proportions of the long corridors and the small poky windows. Tony Manners, one of the consultants, said that the whole place should be knocked down and a new building erected but with the National Health Service hamstrung for lack of funds, where, asked Mr Groom the secretary, was the money going to come from?

Having received a message that he would be glad if I would call on him, I knocked at Dr Felix Coulter's office door. He was the Chairman of the multi-disciplinary committee which was supposed to run the hospital. The Medical Superintendent was now nothing but a memory which dated one – like remembering insulin therapy and using malaria treatment. The committee, of which Dr Coulter was chairman, was suppose to deal with all matters which formerly used to take the Superintendent no more than a day or two but now involved referals to the unwieldy and cumbersome bureaucracy which was strangling the NHS.

Not that Coulter wanted to be chairman. It was a rotating appointment among the consultants with a three-year tenure and, as Manners said, the post was nothing but a headache because you had responsibility without power. Of all the senior doctors Coulter was the best administrator, despite his being executively impotent. Manners was too young, Duggan was too scatterbrained and Paddy Laird was too decent to be tough enough to deal with the plots, cabals and intrigues that went on.

'Ah . . . I wanted to see you. Dr Mullen mentioned the matter to you?'

'Yes,' I said, 'she did mention it to me.'

I disliked Coulter. He was tall and thin with a limp handclasp and the lint-coloured hair and very pale eyes of the albino. There was a slight Canadian twang to his speech because he'd spent several years in Toronto before coming to Barrington Hall as a registrar to Dr Paul Lyle who ran the Addiction Centre. Lyle was a charming Scot who started the unit from nothing and worked so hard at making its reputation that something happened to his inner reserves and he began to lean on morphine and alcohol. Coulter wasn't quite as clever as Lyle, who had written a textbook and several articles containing original thought and material, but he was cool, single-minded and, above all, sober, so when poor Lyle had to be sent on a year's 'sick leave' Coulter fairly leaped from the wings and took over. When Lyle came back, spiritually eviscerated, he found himself without his unit and placed in charge of a block of wards where nothing happened and which were known as a backwater.

'You'd better get stuck in from today. Shouldn't think you'll have any bother. If Duggan could survive then so can you.'

Coulter gave a wintry smile and took off his rimless glasses which he polished with delicate movements of his long white fingers. Manners said Coulter always reminded him of a castrated rabbit and I could see what he meant. There was no warmth or evident humanity in the man. He was a desiccated calculating machine but maybe if he hadn't been, he wouldn't have survived the juggernaut bureaucracy of the endless committees he had to attend. Although he was known as a ruthless and devious liar I sometimes wondered if Coulter didn't suffer not from having an erroneous conscience, but simply from lacking one at all? To call him malicious or spiteful was to impute too human qualities to him. And, after all, he ran the Addiction Centre with ruthless efficiency. He was never going to be destroyed by his own emotional involvement in the poor human wrecks he had to deal with. It was well known that a patient in his charge who had one lapse didn't get the chance to have another one.

'Right, must press on.' Coulter glanced at his watch. How young he looked, I thought, no more than twenty-five. Yet he must be over thirty. 'Your "acting up" as consultant will have to be formerly ratified but that'll be OK. See you.'

And that was that.

I checked with Mrs Bell, my kind and efficient secretary, but she told me that everything was quiet so I decided to go on down to Parker Ward which contained new female cases, those which hadn't yet been properly assessed.

I liked Sister Logan, the middle-aged sister who was in charge. Some people called her too soft, but the patients loved her and having brought up her own family of six helped her to deal with their problems.

'Like some coffee? I hear you've been promoted. Congratulations.'

God, how fast news travels in a hospital, I thought, as Logan went out smiling and Dr Lia Gupta, the registrar, floated in to give her congratulations. She had the pert features of an exquisite Pekingese and was swathed in a peacock and gold sari. Lia might look like the Pearl of the Orient, but she was so bright she'd passed all her postgraduate exams and drove a Morgan with expert but hair-raising speed.

'Mrs Bell has been looking for you,' Lia said. 'You had just left her office apparently.'

An apologetic Mrs Bell told me that St Peter's, the near-by general hospital where I did my outpatients, had an urgent overdose that they wanted me to see, and when could I go?

'I can cope. There isn't anything especially urgent here,' Lia whispered.

I said I'd go in a few minutes and I drank my coffee.

'And we've only got the emergency bed left,' sighed Logan. 'Overdoses, overdoses, and mostly young people.'

And this sounded a serious one, from what Mrs Bell had told me. The girl had swallowed thirty tablets of Paracetamol.

'So dangerous,' Lia said. 'Paracetamol can cause liver damage . . . if they survive.'

'I'd better go,' I said, putting down my cup.

Yes, it had been a struggle to revive Joan Harris, the young staff nurse said when I got to the ward in St Peter's where the woman had been put. It had taken two doctors several hours of work to pull Mrs Harris round and she'd had to spend all of yesterday in the Intensive Care Unit.

'And the beds there are like gold. She is now in one of Mr Madigan's beds and you know how *he* feels about attempted suicides.'

I did indeed. Ned Madigan was an irascible surgeon who believed that people who wanted to kill themselves should be allowed to go ahead, now that it was legal to destroy oneself, and not be taking up valuable time and beds which could be used for more deserving patients.

'A good kick up the backside, that's what they need,' I'd heard him say once.

'This room.' The staff nurse showed me into a narrow little room near her office and I stared at the girl on the bed. She looked so blank and drained that I started to read her notes. Married, with two children; had been suffering from depression for the last five years.

'Well,' I said, sitting down beside her, 'what's the problem then?'

Black hair framed a narrow face which showed not a flicker of animation. Cold, dead eyes, set obliquely, flickered over me. The flat face and the unblinking eyes had a reptilian quality. When she spoke her voice was as chill and flat as her expression.

'There's no problem. I just don't want to live.'

'Why not?'

The thin shoulders lifted in a shrug.

'Why should I? I've been depressed for years now. It gets worse. Nothing helps.'

'I'm here to try to help you. And there are very good tablets now for depression. . . .'

The thin lips parted in a ghost of a smile. 'I've had the lot. Nothing's any good. The only good thing about tablets is that if you take enough they can get you out of life. I just think that life's an obscene joke. I want out.'

I felt irritation. The girl was so fixed and implacable in her hatred and rejection of life that I was beginning to feel my role as a doctor was being questioned.

'What about any worries or fears? Marriage OK?'

I tried to sound calm and not to let my anger show. She gave a hollow laugh.

'My husband's all right. He'd be better without me. And the kids, well, I hammer hell out of Sandra, that's the eldest. I'm afraid I may kill her some day.'

A slight lead there? I tried to probe her a bit more.

'So you'd rather kill yourself instead?'

'I want to kill myself. But not because I love Sandra. I don't love anyone. I don't care for anyone. I can't feel, period.'

'Have you ever felt anything for anyone? I mean, why did you get married?'

'He kept pestering me and I wanted to get away from home. Me Dad was a bastard. And Mum died when I was five. Wore out. She didn't want to die either. But I do. That's what I mean about life being a bloody rotten joke.'

'Don't you think you're being very selfish? Leaving your husband and kids on their own? Everyone feels fed up at times.'

'But not all the time. I've never been happy. Never. And it doesn't get any better. I keep telling you that me husband and the kids will be happier without me. Especially Sandra. I'll make a proper job of it the next time, that's for sure.'

Her eyes bore into mine, fixed, unblinking. I was getting nowhere, not even the merest glimmer of any rapport between us. I was feeling more and more furious and the girl's lips slit into that mirthless smile again. There was no warmth in her, but she was observant.

'I'm making you mad, aren't I? Wasting your time. I heard what that Dr Madigan says about folk who take overdoses, that they need a kick up the arse. Well, he won't get a chance to do that to me.'

'Look,' I said, 'I want you to come into hospital. I don't know whether I can help you but it's my job to have a try.'

'Which hospital? I'm in one, aren't I?'

'Barrington Hall.'

'Christ. The funny farm. No fear. Not there.'

'I can make you,' I said, and explained to her the procedure of putting people on a 'Section' or committal order, which meant that they were obliged to enter hospital for a period of a month at least.

The lips twisted into a travesty of a smile.

'You're not asking me. You're ordering me. I haven't a choice then, have I?'

'Not really.'

There was a small flash of cold rage in her almost lashless eyes and her thin hands knotted together.

'Why the hell can't you leave me alone? Aren't there enough patients for you to see who want to live without wasting your time with such as me? Nothing's going to change my mind. Get that. You tell me I've got to come in so all right I'll come into your bloody nut-house but it won't make any difference. Why can't you all leave me alone? You're not helping me, only salving your own conscience. Piss off.'

She turned away from me, tearless and hopeless, and I was ashamed that I didn't feel more compassion. Maybe it was simply my own ego, the urge for doctors to indulge their God complex, but I felt I had to do something; I couldn't stand by and let this girl snuff herself out without at least trying to help. I wouldn't succeed. I was certain of that. But I'd have a try.

'Tough cookie, isn't she?' Like policemen, the young housemen were getting younger and younger and the tousle-haired youth in the flapping white coat with a stethoscope slung around his neck looked about sixteen.

'Send her to Parker Ward,' I told him, and then realized that it wasn't a 'him' but a pixie-faced girl.

'What can you do for her?' asked Dr Pansy Drew as she introduced herself.

'That's just what I'm wondering myself,' I replied.

5

I was so upset by my failure at achieving anything therapeutic with Joan Harris that I decided to call and see Frankie and Barney that evening. A murky autumnal fog swirled around the house, making it look more dismal than ever, but Barney, looking glowingly healthy in well-cut tweeds, answered the door with Willy yapping at his heels. Frankie was due in at any moment he told me, and pressed a very large gin into my hands. He threw another log on the huge fire and refilled his own glass from a bottle of very special whisky.

He beamed and referred fondly to Frankie. 'Works far too hard you know. She's exploited by that bloody hospital, just as you are, and as for that Cousins, well what can you expect of a fellow who got out of doing military service because of hammer toes?'

He made no reference to his throat, and as usual when he was in a good humour he seemed to be able to hear perfectly. In fact he looked the picture of contentment, and if I didn't know him so well I'd have been astounded at the Lazarus-like way he'd risen from his sick bed. He must have seen my eyes popping because he lay back on his wing-backed chair and tilted his profile so that I got the benefit of his good side. He was very vain about his appearance, and Frankie always described his sojourns in the bathroom as being like Marie Antoinette giving herself a *grande toilette*. His white hair formed an aureole around his rather cherubic face and his blue eyes glittered with bonhomie and whisky.

'I expect you see a great change in me,' he said, waving a very white handkerchief which seemed to be impregnated with some deliciously herb-like scent. 'I've inherited a very strong constitution from my father's side you know. And a good thing, too, or I'd have to depend on you people. Indeed, I generally feel so well that I find time hanging heavy on my hands. One can read, listen to music and visit art galleries and museums but the depressing part of growing old is that one runs out of contemporaries. There are so few people left with whom one can have a worth-while exchange of ideas. Now that's one of the things that attracted me to Frances. I was astounded at her knowledge of the arts . . . amazed at her familiarity with literature . . .'

I wondered what he'd say if he knew that Frankie had told me she was equally amazed at his knowledge of the arts and that she'd guessed he couldn't have done a damn thing in the army except read. As Barney rhapsodied on about the virtues of Frankie, his tongue loosened and lubricated by frequent refills of his glass, I was hard put to it to remember the roaring exchange between the two of them last night. I couldn't help speculating on their sex life. I knew they slept together because Frankie had often told me about Barney's snoring and his curses when he tripped going to the lavatory at night.

'He says I've brought back feelings he's not had for years,' she told me once. 'Rejuvenated his libido.'

The fire was soporific and the gin had been a double one so I lay back on the comfortable chesterfield and listened to Barney who was now launched on a series of risqué but very funny stories.

With one of his disconcerting changes of mood he looked at the clock and said angrily, 'It's after nine o'clock. Now what could Frankie be doing? She's not on night duty unless that bugger Cousins has conned her into extra work. It's no use talking to her. No use at all. She'll listen to anyone except me. Did you know that Cousins runs an abortion clinic in the West End? Mrs Marley the cleaning woman told me that. Oh, yes. And there's talk of him having a mistress as well. Wouldn't trust that fellow to hold my overcoat. You don't think he's got his sights on Frankie do you?'

His blue eyes blazed and I assured him that no, no I didn't think so at all. Frankie had much better taste, I told him. It wasn't Frankie, he added, but Cousins' lechery that he distrusted.

Just then there was the sound of a key turning in the front

door and Frankie appeared wrapped in a plum-coloured cape which she flung off in a dramatic gesture to reveal a matching dress. She unwound a pale pink scarf from her neck, said how glad she was to see me, and kissed Barney with affection.

'Hungry anybody?' she asked. I said no and Barney told her how much he'd enjoyed the cold duck and salad she'd left for him and that we both must have some of the very special white wine he'd kept chilled for her return.

'Lovely darling. God, what a day.' Frankie sprawled on a chair and kicked off her shoes. Her ankles were very puffy.

'And how did you get on, Joyce?' she asked as she sipped her drink, and Barney hovered lovingly near her. They were looking at each other with the rapt attention of two young lovers. But Frankie's foot kept tapping on the floor and she flicked the ash off her cigarette in short quick taps, a way she had when she had something on her mind. When I was telling her about Joan Harris I became increasingly aware that she was distinctly preoccupied in spite of her apparent attention.

'One has so much time,' she said as Barney refilled her glass, 'and this girl seems absolutely determined to kill herself. What can you do? Go through some motions, that's all. I don't agree with Madigan's attitude, but, damn it, we have our work cut out to try and help those who want to be helped without trying to stop people who've made up their minds to destroy themselves. You've got to have sense as well as sensibility, Joyce. I had a girl in the surgery tonight and she said she'd throw herself in the river if I didn't get her an abortion because she wanted to wear her bikini in the South of France.'

'Let the buggers go to hell,' said Barney. 'Can't stand people holding a gun to my head.' He stood in front of the fire which was now an inferno and Willy snored and snorted with the heat until he moved his bulk to a cooler spot under the chair.

'Well, I've brought my girl in,' I said rather defiantly. 'At least if I don't help her I'll feel I've tried.'

'Can I get you another drink, darling?' Frankie asked and Barney passed her his glass. He looked almost beatific and patted Frankie's shoulder benignly as she passed him on her way to the drinks table.

'I was looking at my salary chit today,' she sighed. 'It's ghastly what they take off us in tax.'

'We'll be reduced to carrying money in suitcases soon,' Barney said. 'Just like the Weimar Republic.'

'Yes, you have to snatch at every chance to supplement your income,' Frankie went on. 'Every chance.'

This gave me a clue to the reason for the far away look in her eyes. She was Kerry enough not to come out with a stark statement, but it was evident to me that she was giving Barney the softening up treatment.

'The husband of a patient of mine has offered me something which wouldn't take much time and which pays very well,' she began.

'Is there money in it? Is that what you're saying? Speak up, can't you?' What with the heat and the drink and the excitement which money always induced in him, Barney's hearing mechanism appeared to be getting affected.

'There is,' said Frankie, stretching herself like a large cat. 'It involves answering readers' queries in a magazine. No more than that.'

'What magazine?' I asked.

'*Urge*,' said Frankie. 'You've heard of it?'

Of course I had. It was a high-class pornographic periodical with a huge circulation whose cover depicted incredible variations on bottoms, breasts and phalluses.

'Yes. It's a sex magazine. But all I'd have to do would be to answer readers' queries, strictly anonymously of course.'

'Whose idea was this? Cousins?' Barney shouted. 'I expect he takes the photographs for it. Have you gone mad? What about your professional reputation?'

'That doesn't pay the bills. And neither does my salary or your pension,' Frankie said. 'I'm taking it. Why shouldn't I? My name won't appear and all I do is to collect the money.'

'Christ how low can you sink?' Barney rasped. 'A lady doctor writing for a sex rag? So this is what the medical profession has come to.'

'Yes,' shouted Frankie, 'and if you read the medical journals you'll see that doctors are having to sell knickers and Marks and

30

Spencer shirts and even take in bloody lodgers because none of us can live on our rotten salaries.'

'And what skill and expertise have you got that you should be picked on for this noble task?' Barney had turned puce and his drink dribbled from the shaking hand holding his glass. 'Why should they pick on you?'

'"They" didn't pick on me. I just happen to have a patient whose husband edits this magazine.'

'Oh, I see.' Barney gave a cold laugh. 'And she thought you looked the type who'd be able to advise all the perverts who read and write to this sort of filthy rag.'

'Look, Barney,' Frankie said, 'I'm not going to act in a blue movie or run a new-style brothel. I'm simply going to send anonymous answers to people who probably are just like my own patients. I don't see anything wrong in it and I'm going to do it. Don't you think it's all right, Joyce?'

I didn't see anything really wrong in it, just wondered at Frankie's energy and initiative and wished that I'd got the chance myself. It sounded an interesting assignment.

'Of course,' sneered Barney. 'You're a woman of the world, a woman of experience. I suppose your past will help you, won't it?'

'Oh, shut up. You sound like something out of a Victorian melodrama,' Frankie said.

'I see. I see,' Barney said, well goaded now. 'Oh, I know I'm an old fogey, an anachronism in your world. I wonder why you bother with me when my views are so dated. I suppose I should be delighted to have you whoring on paper?'

'Oh, for Christ's sake,' Frankie groaned. 'Whores, harlots, scarlet women, people don't bloody talk that way any more, Barney.'

Barney drew himself up. He was about a foot shorter than Frankie, but from years of drilling, his back was very straight and he held his drink with stern dignity.

'And what is so wrong with being ladylike?' he asked.

'Because I'm not a bloody lady. I'm a peasant. You knew that when you took up with me, you sod.'

'What's she saying? She knows I can't hear when she shouts?'

31

Barney turned to me, playing his trump card.

'Don't come that,' Frankie, maddened, yelled. 'Sure your own father was in the fish trade so don't come The Gent act with me. No bloody lady could stand you. Well, I'm going to start this job tomorrow so stick that in your pipe if it isn't blocked.'

So much for my evening of relaxation I thought, as Barney, after an icy look at Frankie and a distant nod to me, stalked out followed by the waddling Willy. Then he came back and announced, looking at the ceiling, 'I shall not be in tomorrow. I am meeting a friend.'

He went out and Frankie laughed. 'That'll be old Sullivan, a retired judge who was a buddy of Barney's in India. They'll get sozzled and moan about women. Sullivan was married three times and now lives with his housekeeper. Had four children by her, too, and he in his seventies. Barney'll come round. As long as there's money in it.'

'Suppose anyone from Barrington Hall finds out, Frankie?' I asked as she began to turn out lights and empty ash trays.

'I don't give a damn,' she said. 'As long as the money comes in, kid, I don't give a shit.'

I believed her. Anyone like Frankie, who had left her red pants behind the screen in a doctor's room, and then telephoned him next day about it, wasn't the one to be sensitive to others' opinions!

6

Next morning Mrs Bell told me that two calls for domiciliary visits had come in. One was to a Mrs Bird who lived in Waterloo Road, Yorkely, which was about five miles from the hospital, and the other, to a Mrs Pillsworth, was in Varley Road, Haston. Haston was in the opposite direction to Yorkely which meant I'd have to brave the dreaded Macaroni Junction. Engineers and city planners were justly proud of the mass of flyovers, lanes and underpasses which comprised the junction, but even travelling through it as a passenger gave me palpitations, but I'd have to make a start, I couldn't keep on getting taxis. So after kind Mrs Bell had done her best to brief me with maps, diagrams and verbal instructions, I set off in my battered Mini, muscles in spasm and damp hands gripping the steering wheel. What would happen if I got stuck in the wrong lane and found myself careering towards London or northwards towards Newcastle? Or nearly as bad, if I strayed on to one of those lanes which drove right through the city on to one of those ghastly ring roads which seemed to go on forever?

Feeling as if I'd mastered the Matterhorn I managed to get to Yorkely and began to drive through endless streets of sleazy shops selling garishly cheap clothes, dusty looking establishments selling rickety ancient furniture or cheap modern stuff. Almost every second store had an Indian name over it, and the streets milled with Asians whose bright vivid clothes contrasted with the drabness of the district.

I pulled in the car and after much thumbing over the map I found that I was only two blocks away from Waterloo Road. My face in the driving mirror looked ravaged and I did my best to assume some vestige of professional calm. I couldn't imagine Mrs Bird feeling more wobbly than I did after I'd negotiated

Macaroni Junction.

Actually, Waterloo Road was a pleasant little row of Victorian houses, and the woman who opened the door looked as fresh and clean as if she'd just sprung out of the bath and given herself a facial.

'Mrs Bird?'

'Who are you? Who sent you?'

She was a good-looking woman with a dark gypsyish handsome face, but her voice rose several shrieking decibels and I was very glad when her large lumbering husband appeared.

'Now then, Alice, this is the lady doctor come to help you. Tell her about all them ideas you been having about the gas coming through the letter box and the police bugging your bedroom.'

Mrs Bird adjusted her white turban over her dark hair, turned on her trim heels and walked rapidly to the back of the bright clean kitchen which was dominated by a large washing machine.

'If she can't smell the gas then she's a bloody fool, and I bet the police have sent her round to do more wiring. I'm not talking to her. I got washing to do.'

She began to fire clothes into the vast machine which revved up like a jet engine, and when she rushed out to the line in the yard to collect more washing Mr Bird said to me, 'This happened to her five year ago and old Doctor Spencer brought her into hospital and treated her and she come right as rain, but the death of her Dad last week's brought all the queer ideas back. She needs to come into hospital, Doc.'

I could see that. Gas and bugging and the mad aggression in Mrs Bird's flashing dark eyes meant a paranoid psychosis. But it was unlikely she'd come in of her own accord, so I'd probably have to do a section on her.

The door opened and Mrs Bird staggered in carrying a basket of washing, which she began to shake fiercely. Then there was a pattering sound, and an enormous Alsatian dog raced towards me. I thought I was going to be torn to bits and my yell seemed to quieten Mrs Bird, who suddenly called to the dog in a quiet voice and he padded outside.

'Is he dangerous, Mrs Bird?' I panted, and she clicked her heels like a Spanish dancer and flashed a smile at me.

'Only when he bites,' she answered.

Then she made a pot of tea.

It was as if the wicked-looking dog appearing and my obvious terror had been cathartic for Mrs Bird, because after plying me with tea she agreed to come into hospital if I gave an undertaking to speak to the Chief Constable about the gas and bugging!

Mr Bird, sagging with relief, came out to the car with me, and such was his gratitude at my taking his wife in that he offered to direct me to Haston which was a new housing estate further on from Varley. But I was so delighted in having navigated so well thus far, I thanked him but declined his offer and set off for Haston on my own. It must have been the effect of the Alsatian's almost-attack or my inability to find Varley Road on the map, but I got hopelessly lost and soon found myself back near the hospital. My pride wouldn't allow me to go in and ask Mrs Bell to set me on my way. After further fruitless mulling over my map, I asked a few people where Haston was but two said they'd never heard of it and the third said he'd heard of it but couldn't direct me. I was about to concede defeat and check with Mrs Bell when I stopped and asked an intelligent-looking Indian who was stalking along looking scholarly and carrying a briefcase and umbrella.

'Certainly I have heard of Haston and the road called Varley. I will show you exactly,' he said politely.

He was so mannerly and courteous that I didn't like to say anything when he opened the car door and arranged himself beside me with his briefcase on his knees and his dark eyes glinting with pleasure behind his rimless spectacles.

We set off, him directing me with easy confidence, and in between, giving his views on the political situation in Pakistan, the state of the pound, the violence in modern society and whether capital punishment should be brought back. He was obviously a very intelligent man and he informed me that he worked as a clerk in a firm of solicitors, but was at present recovering from an illness.

The sun burst out in the sudden disconcerting dazzle that early autumn sometimes shows, and Mr Singh sighed with poetic delight and waved his slender hands at the orange and gold trees in the park we were passing by.

'Ah, to contemplate the beauties and bounties of nature,' he mused. 'What is that one of your bards says, "Season of mists and mellow fruitfulness"? Is it not delightful to be able to avail of modern technology in the form of the automobile so that we can drive around like this observing the human condition and appreciating the weather? Very lovely.'

He sat hunched beside me and stared contentedly out of the window. He was a very nice man, with the rather dated good manners that Indians often have, but time was getting on, although it seemed to mean nothing to Mr Singh.

I reminded him that we had been driving for well over an hour now, and although the part of the city which we were driving through was a pleasant one, full of large well-built houses, leafy roads and well-kept parks, I hadn't noticed any familiar roads at all, and again I asked Mr Singh if he was sure he knew where Varley Road, Haston, was.

'Most certainly I do,' he beamed. 'We will be getting to it presently. Meantime let us enjoy the last vestiges of good weather before winter has us in its grip. What a good driver you are, madam. Really most expert. And so very kind. It is really jolly nice to have such pleasant companionship.'

Mr Singh's eyes were so limpidly sincere and his sing-song voice so full of genuine emotion that I couldn't take offence at his flowery compliments, but I was beginning to get very impatient, and after two hours I was so tired that I almost went through a red light. Mr Singh didn't appear to notice but was humming a Bengali song to himself.

Suddenly something snapped in me and I drew the car into a lay-by and said that really I couldn't go on. I was weary and exhausted and I had to tell Mr Singh that I was a doctor and had to get to Haston to call on a patient.

'A doctor?' Mr Singh said. 'Very nice. I myself am unfortunately in the hands of your noble and ancient profession at the moment. Yes, indeed. They are doing wonders for me.'

A terrible idea was beginning to take root in my brain. I'd picked Mr Singh up near Barrington Hall. He obviously hadn't a clue where Haston was, but had conned me into giving him an afternoon's joy ride and I'd been crazy enough to allow him to use me as his chauffeur.

'Yes. I am at present in hospital,' Mr Singh said gently.

'Which one?'

'Barrington Hall. Doctor Raschid is my doctor.'

Oh God, I thought, if Raschid ever heard of this I could imagine his screams of laughter. To pick up a patient as a navigator, especially when it was patently clear that that patient hadn't the least idea of direction! I could only hope that Singh would keep his mouth shut, and so I restrained my rage and said that I was sorry we couldn't continue our ride and would Mr Singh kindly get out at the next bus stop and let me get on with my call?

'Certainly madam,' he said. 'Most certainly. And I must thank you for such a very pleasant and lovely ride. So very kind of you.'

I had two strokes of luck because very shortly after that I came across a bus stop and got Mr Singh to alight. He doffed his hat, bowed, thanked me again and joined the waiting people looking like a scholarly Brahmin as he took out some papers from his case and peered at them intently.

Then I saw a Panda car with two friendly policemen in it. Perhaps I looked so red and hot and distrait or maybe they hadn't much to do, but they told me to follow them and we drove directly to number 128 Varley Road.

'Better go now. Neighbours are always nosey when they see us drive up,' one of the young policemen said, and the car shot off before I could thank them properly.

The lady who opened the door, Mrs Pillsworth, was dressed in a frilly low-cut ensemble, very high heeled shoes and a floppy hat wavering on her brassy blonde hair. She greeted me with the effusive euphoria of the person suffering from mania, quite the opposite to the cross and paranoid Mrs Bird.

'Come in, dear. Dr King said you were coming. Oh, it's all go, isn't it? Rush, rush, rush.'

I followed her into a small but comfortable parlour crammed with bric-a-brac and knick-knacks. The walls were plastered with photographs of a smiling and slimmer Mrs Pillsworth clutching a man in Air Force uniform, and the shelves and mantelpiece were cluttered with china ornaments.

'I love nice things,' Mrs Pillsworth said. 'That's why I can't understand who's been stealing my clothes. I have no slip, no pants . . . look . . .'

She tore open her dress to reveal nothing but flabby bare flesh. A ferret faced little woman who had come in grabbed me when Mrs Pillsworth went out to make tea, and told me that she, Mrs Naylor, was a neighbour, and Mrs Pillsworth was a widow and her two children were in the States.

'Bonkers she is. I seen it coming,' Mrs Naylor said. 'A nice poor soul when she's well, but there's no stopping her when she's like this. She's spending money she hasn't got. Talking rubbish to everyone and wandering out at night. The police had to bring her back twice, and she's taken to going down to the local school at assembly and sitting on the rostrum with the teachers and of course they don't like it. But the poor thing used to be a teacher herself.'

'It's too much bother making tea,' Mrs Pillsworth flounced in, bearing two glasses, 'so I've brought you a glass of my dandelion wine. So refreshing!'

It wasn't refreshing. It was vile, but I thought it better to humour Mrs Pillsworth, who chattered ceaselessly, racing from subject to subject in the disjointed tangential way that manics have. With her blazing eyes, flushed cheeks and ceaseless jumping up and down to re-arrange an ornament or show us a photograph, I could believe Mrs Naylor when, after Mrs Pillsworth had teetered out to show us a blouse she'd just bought, she told me that the poor woman hadn't been sleeping or eating for days and was full of what Mr Bird at Yorkely had called 'queer ideas'. Indeed by comparison with Mrs Pillsworth, Mrs Bird seemed almost sane.

When Mrs Pillsworth re-appeared she was dressed in a shortie nightgown made for a slim young girl which looked obscenely grotesque on Mrs Pillsworth's wobbly, veiny limbs.

'I'm a hot cross bun,' she said, pirouetting around and starting to do a sort of lumbering minuet.

Mrs Naylor rolled her eyes at me in resignation, and I said that I'd like Mrs Pillsworth to come into hospital 'for a rest'.

38

She was delighted. Her brain, always active, was now racing, she said, and she had so many wonderful and unusual experiences that they amounted to inspiration, and she'd like to write them down. A rest in hospital would give her the opportunity to put down her thoughts for posterity.

'I'll bring you over in a taxi, Elsie,' Mrs Naylor said. 'Sooner the better.'

'Oh what a beautiful morning,' Mrs Pillsworth roared and then rushed upstairs, to get ready, she said.

'Thank God for that,' Mrs Naylor said. 'The walls are thin in these houses, and the row she's kicked up every night's been terrible and my husband's a man who must get his sleep. You'd be having me in as a patient if you didn't take her. I'd better go and see where she's gone.'

Mrs Naylor was back in a few minutes, after there was the sound of raised voices in the hall and the slam of the front door.

'She's on about having no pants,' she said, 'and she's got drawers full of them cause she's very particular when she's well, but now she says she's got to go across the road and borrow some from Mrs Barrow. And *she* won't be pleased because she's a Plymouth Brethren and thinks Mrs P is possessed with evil spirits.'

I was filled with gloom that Mrs Pillsworth's mania might drive her off on some other mission, but fortunately she arrived back in five minutes waving two pairs of what used to be called 'directoire knickers' and said that she was now ready to go.

'H'm,' Mrs Naylor said, with a certain sardonic humour as Mrs Pillsworth, with all the lack of modesty of the very unbalanced, pulled on the bilious green knickers over her plump hips. 'She'll come to no harm in *those*. Good as a pair of concrete pants I should think. Come on then, Elsie. Doctor's got other calls.'

Doctor hadn't, but doctor felt so tired that by the time home was reached bed seemed more important than food and I slept till nine o'clock the following morning.

7

'Wasn't too bad was it?' asked Mrs Bell when I went in to dictate some letters next morning.

'No, no, I found my way all right,' I lied. To try and explain about careering around for over two hours with a Barrington patient would be just too much, with a grapevine system more sensitive than those operating in most mental hospitals.

'Well, Dr Morgan would like you to go and visit what he describes as a "geriatric alcoholic". She's over eighty and apparently bullies her unmarried son, who lives with her, into buying her at least one bottle, and sometimes two, of the best brandy every day.'

I decided to ring John Morgan. He had a practice quite locally and was a good and hard working GP who had a concern for his patients and didn't often bother calling in psychiatrists. I wondered how on earth he thought I was going to wean a brandy-soaked old lady off what was probably a tipple of many years' standing, and anyway, if she could afford brandy, wasn't it as good a way to go as any? Pickled in the best product of the grape! Especially when to be old was to be unwanted, as so many of the elderly were daily reminded.

'Ah but it's not Mrs Matty Rossiter I'm worried about,' John Morgan explained when I phoned him. 'First of all her son says that the money is running out because she'll only drink Courvoisier, and secondly she's such an old bully that her continual niggling is getting him down to the extent that I think he's near breaking point. She's as tough as old boots, though I think she's beginning to dement a bit now. Mind you, the son is a bit soft, but he's so brutalized by her bullying that all his will is sapped now and it's as much as he can do to look after his mother and get out to buy brandy. If he refuses to go she stands at the window and yells, or wallops him with her stick. By the way, she's a religious maniac, a fanatical Catholic, and the only one who has any influence over her is Father Mortimer.'

I knew Father Mortimer, a delightful Woosterish Benedictine parish priest who had given up a baronetcy to become a monk. With his rubicund face and plummy voice you might be fooled into thinking the man was a fool until you realized that behind the Edwardian panache there was a cool and clever brain.

He couldn't be there himself, Morgan went on, because he had a very difficult obstetric case to deal with, but if I could get around this morning Father Mortimer would be there.

'I don't expect you'll be able to do much,' Morgan said apologetically, 'but I do feel that the son needs a bit of support.'

'Mind you, if he, the son, came into hospital, his mother couldn't get the brandy and she'd probably die,' I said.

'You've got to be joking,' Morgan said. 'The old girl's got lots of other mugs ready to keep up the supplies.'

There was one good thing about it, Mrs Rossiter lived quite near the hospital in a crumbling old house near a disused railway station. When I was parking the car I happened to look up at one of the top windows which was open and I saw a scrawny old woman, white hair tumbling around her witch-like features and nightgown flapping around her gaunt body, shouting the most horrible obscenities.

'Terrible isn't it?' a stout little woman carrying a shopping basket said to me as I walked up towards the house. 'It's old Mrs Rossiter bawling for her brandy again. She ought to be put away. It's a disgrace. Children listening to the like of that and her pretending to be such a holy woman. Her son is a saint, that's what I think.'

The man who opened the door after I had pressed the rusty old bell for ages looked nearly as old as his mother. He had the same thin features and nutcracker jaw. His hair was grey and his pallid colour and skinny body indicated malnutrition.

'You'll be Doctor Delaney,' he said. 'I'm so glad you've come. She's at it again. I haven't been able to get out yet for more brandy, you see. Excuse the mess. This way. . . .'

'Mess' was an inadequate word to describe the faded filth of

41

the Rossiter house. I could see a dark damp kitchen with a dusty old range at the end of the fusty hall, and as we climbed the stairs which were covered in discoloured matting, I noticed that the wallpaper was peeling and there were damp patches everywhere.

'Get into bed, Mother, a lady doctor's come to see you.'

The old woman hopped away from the window and glared at me. The walls of the smelly room were covered with garish pictures of saints and martyrs and there were several statues on the dirty mantelpiece. I noticed two dry Holy Water fonts fastened to the wall near the tumbled bed. The blankets were thin and grey and the sheets were stained and obviously responsible for some of the smell in the room. Over the unmade bed there was a huge picture, appallingly badly painted, of a thunderous looking God perched on a cloud surrounded by obese angels, and pointing dramatically to writhing penitents who were obviously suffering the Last Judgement. On the shaky old bamboo table by the bed were several empty brandy bottles and some boxes of pills.

'Who is she? I don't want to see her. Get her out and get down to the shops for my brandy. What have you come to my house uninvited for? What with the ghastly meals on wheels which even my dog refuses, the Social Service snoopers and Mournful Morgan, I get nothing but busybodies. I don't go into other people's houses, so why can't they keep out of mine?'

There was a certain logic to this and the old woman's son – whose name was Jonathan, he told me – poured some brandy from some secret cache in the landing and waved it at his mother.

'Back to bed and you get this, Mother,' he said.

The old lady switched like a rabbit and pattered back to her tousled bed. She grabbed the glass of brandy from her son and after downing half of it with a much steadier hand than Ignatius O'Halloran she cocked a clear blue eye at Jonathan and said,

'That's not Courvoisier. It's bloody cheap Hennessy again.'

To try and divert her, as she tossed back the last of the liquid, I asked her why she had been shouting and waving her arms at the window and she said regally,

'I wasn't "shouting and waving" you stupid woman. I love music and I was merely conducting the "Eroica" to cheer myself up because I'd run out of brandy. Which reminds me. Get down to the shops, Jonathan!'

'I will if you'll talk to Dr Delaney,' Jonathan said with excellent timing. 'And I'll get the very best Courvoisier,' he added with the air of a conjurer producing a very superior type of rabbit from the best of top hats.

'Oh, all right then,' Mrs Rossiter said, and stared at me with unblinkingly piercing blue eyes. 'I suppose you're one of the modern people who think it's clever not to believe in God?'

Thank God for a convent education I thought as I told her that I was a Catholic and had been educated by the Ursulines.

'Never liked them,' she said. 'Prissy. I prefer the Little Sisters of the Poor myself.'

There was the sound of the front door slamming and Mrs Rossiter closed one eye conspiratorially.

'If you search in the third drawer of the dressing-table you'll find a small bottle of brandy wrapped in a petticoat. Bring it to me. Iron Rations.'

Her alcohol level seemed to be continually topped up and I didn't see that much harm could come to her by another tot or two, so I scrabbled amongst the faded and mothball smelling underclothes until I found the brandy bottle and brought it back to the old woman. She didn't even wait for it to be poured into one of the dull-looking glasses by the bed but lifted it to her toothless mouth and dribbled it down her stringy throat. Then she slid the bottle under the torn old pillow.

'What are you then?' she asked. The beaky nose, sharp chin and penetrating eyes gave her a disconcertingly hawk-like appearance and although she looked all of her eighty-seven years the brandy didn't seem to have affected her brain.

'I'm a psychiatrist,' I said, and she snatched out the remains of the brandy and swigged it, after which she stared at me and snorted, 'Can't solve your own problems and you set yourself up to try and solve others'.'

She really was a rude old bitch I thought, and I felt so cross with her bossing and boozing that I said, 'At least I don't swig brandy all day and terrorize my son to buy liquor you can't either of you afford.'

I saw her blotchy old hand reach for the thick stick by the side of her bed and I ducked back in time to avoid a whack on the face.

'What do you know about me? Or about my son? You march in here like all the rest of the do-gooders, and you get horrified and revolted and make all sorts of suggestions because it gives all of you such a lovely warm glow of being holier than I am. Well, you don't know enough to judge. You psychiatrists have taken the place of God to the Godless, the despairing and the stupid. But, leave *Him to judge me*. I'll meet Him soon enough.'

She gasped and spluttered and tipped the almost empty brandy bottle down her throat.

'Let me tell you something,' she went on. 'I only began to drink five years ago. I've been a widow for twenty years and my son is an epileptic. Maybe you think that's a reason for me to stop drinking, but I can't bear to see him during his fits. I have no friends because I've never been a very nice character. Too direct, too abrupt. Somebody once said that I was like a heavy meal when what most people want is a digestible collation. Brandy makes everything easier. I haven't the courage to commit suicide you see, so I do it the coward's way. There's enough money for the liquor to see me out. And for Tom.'

She closed her eyes and looked like a tired eagle. No, I hadn't known the facts. She wasn't the dramatic type, and as she said, too direct to invent lies, so what she said was true. As she lay like a stricken old bird, I tried to imagine what it would be like to have to lie here in this stinking room surrounded by bad religious art, with no friends and an epileptic son.

Her eyes opened and she said clearly, 'So don't think you're going to commit me to a mental hospital. I shall die here amongst the dust and the dirt and the brandy will blur it a bit. . . .'

Her voice trailed off and I thought she'd fallen asleep, but when Jonathan came in bearing a bottle of Courvoisier and accompanied by Father Mortimer she reared up in the bed, eyes sparkling and slack old mouth open for the glass of brandy her son poured for her.

'And how are you, Matilda, my dear?' Father Mortimer nodded to me and sat down on the edge of Mrs Rossiter's bed watching her gulping back her brandy.

'Surviving unfortunately. I've just been telling this lady psychiatrist that she's not going to put me away. There's too much of that. It's as if the old have the Black Plague today. You can serve sex with the soup but put away the old. They remind people too much of morality. Any lunatic can stay out in the community now but we old ones are to be stuffed away where the sight of us won't offend people. Oh yes, euthanasia will come, but I prefer this way. . . .'

Watched by the priest, her son and myself she raised her glass with a steady hand, and then putting down the glass she asked Father Mortimer to pray for her and said that now she wanted to sleep, please.

As we crept out of the room, while Jonathan remained to pull the threadbare blankets over his mother, Father Mortimer sighed and said, 'I think it's easier for the senile you know. They're spared so much.'

I nodded. The old woman had spoken such terrible truths. But what about Jonathan?

'I've arranged for him to go for a long holiday to one of our monasteries in Devon . . . when the time comes,' Father Mortimer said.

At the gate he looked back at the rambling old house and said: 'You know, I'm sure St Peter will not only let Mrs Rossiter through but I wouldn't be surprised if he didn't have a bottle of Courvoisier ready for her.'

8

'Mr Harris would like a word with you,' Sister Logan said when I managed to find time to go up to Parker Ward where Joan Harris had been admitted the night before. 'He's waiting outside. Doesn't look as if he appreciates how ill his wife is.'

That was an understatement. Mr Harris was a squat little man in his late forties dressed in dungarees and wearing a fatuous smile on his chubby face.

I tried to be gentle but direct. When I explained that Joan simply didn't want to live or accept any treatment he just beamed and said she'd always had 'black moods' and was very 'self willed'.

It was more than that, I persisted; Mrs Harris had every intention of trying to commit suicide again and, worse than that, there was the danger to the children.

'Oh, they're all right,' he said; 'they're with Gran at the moment and she loves having 'em.'

Why on earth had Joan married a man who, to put it kindly, had such a low IQ and, to be unkind, was positively thick? Maybe it was that she cared so little about her life and destiny that she simply married, as she'd said, the first male who'd offered her the chance of getting away from what sounded a pretty traumatic home.

'Yes, everything'll be all right, Doc,' went on Harris. 'I'd like her out for the week-end. That'll buck her up. Give her a few bevvies Saturday night and she'll be fine. She can be a star turn when she wants, can Joan.'

I tried to explain to him again that his wife was an ill woman and that she wasn't fit to leave hospital, that I could stop her from going and that I didn't think a 'few bevvies' were going to do anything for her deep melancholy.

It was like trying to stop the Niagara Falls with a plank. Indeed Mr Harris himself was like a plank. I gave up. If Joan was determined to kill herself, and I knew she was, then she could do it inside the hospital as well as outside and neither I nor anyone else could stop her.

'I'll keep her tablets, believe me, Doc. And take her to see the kids. Just to see them. Please let her go.'

He gave another reassuring grin and when Logan came in I told her that I was letting Joan Harris out on week-end leave. She raised her eyebrows but after Harris had gone out she said we couldn't keep the girl under surveillance for ever and anyway the children, who after all were the primary consideration, were in safe hands.

'Unless she takes them away from her mother-in-law,' I said gloomily. I was glad when Frankie rang to say that she was free for lunch and could I meet her in the hospital canteen at one?

'I'll be there,' I said. 'And bring a copy of *Urge*. How are you doing?' I asked.

'Fine. I wondered where the sex changers, flashers and deviants had gone. I know now. They're all flourishing but they've deserted us shrinkies for the porn mags.'

I went along to see Joan Harris and tell her that I was allowing her out for the week-end. She lay staring disinterestedly out of the window, thin shoulders hunched, and you could almost smell her sadness.

'Joan, I've been talking to your husband,' I said, 'and I'm letting you out for a day, maybe the week-end.'

The curious eyes flickered in my direction and there was the hint, the merest suggestion, of a smile from her pale lips.

'That will be nice,' she said.

The flat cliché infuriated me. Damn it, couldn't she show some quiver of emotion at the thought of possibly seeing her children?

'Aren't you pleased at seeing the kids?' I fumed. 'Don't you think we're showing trust in you to let you out after all your overdosing?'

'What am I supposed to do?' She folded her narrow arms at the back of her head. 'Touch my forelock, curtsey and say "Yes, thank you very much, Doctor." You're not Gods, you doctors. Not any more you aren't.'

'Don't be dramatic,' I said. 'Your husband said you could be a star turn and he's right.'

'Well what's the bloody point of you coming along asking me bloody silly questions about whether I feel all right when I keep telling you that I *can't* feel. I can't feel nothing for no one and it makes you bloody mad because you're like God and you think you should be able to make me feel better with your magic powers only you can't and it makes you bloody furious. There aren't any Happy Pills you see, and if there were you haven't got them.'

I could have rushed at her and shaken her till she rattled. But mad as I was, I felt we were getting somewhere, this strange girl and I. Her show of anger was better than her morbid apathy, and although I was pricked in a sensitive clinical spot by her tart reminder that the God-like doctor days were gone, maybe she wasn't so wrong after all and maybe my concern for her wasn't so much altruistic as a boost to my own ego as the Great Physician?

My anger disappeared and we stared at each other like two wary warriors.

'Promise me you won't try another overdose,' I said.

'Can't do that. But I'll promise to try. Sorry for saying "bloody" so much but doctors make me feel like that.'

*   *   *

Frankie, looking like a stout gypsy rather than a doctor, was already eating her lunch when I reached the canteen shortly after one. She greeted me with one hand whilst the other one was engaged in pouring cream on chocolate gâteau. Calories were of less than academic interest to Frankie for whom several crash diets had reduced her blood sugar and increased her temper but had done nothing about her girth. Sex appeal didn't depend on weight, she told me; after all, the voluptuous Emma Hamilton hadn't done so bad for herself.

'Here,' she said, passing me a magazine with a cover on it like

48

an anatomist gone mad. It was typical of Frankie that she hadn t even bothered to wrap the magazine in something and I was terrified that a crowd of young nurses at the next table would get an eyeful.

The writhing, coiling and twisting couples on the cover of the magazine had certainly obeyed its title 'Urge'. There were bosoms of every size, shape, contour and position, testicles like prize melons and penises like gigantic marrows. Every outsize organ was being crammed into unusual orifices, and when I flicked the magazine open the titles of the articles were just as fleshy as the cover. 'Drugs for Droop', 'Loosen and Lubricate', 'Throw out your vibrator and pleasure yourself'.

'The usual stuff,' said Frankie with the sang-froid I'd always envied in her. It was as if she'd managed a sophisticated brothel for years.

'Here's a few of the readers' letters passed on to me for answering. They're rather sad some of them.'

I thought that most of them were tragic. A squadron-leader wrote to say that he was obsessed with the female derrière and spent valuable time 'chasing likely ones'. 'My wife is a good sport but unfortunately objects to donning the attire of a deep sea diver which would enhance my sexual pleasure.' 'Where can I find a non-professional lady, and it must be a lady, to thrash me regularly?'

'I wouldn't have a clue how to go about answering these,' I said wonderingly.

'You would at fifty quid a time,' she said, calmly helping herself to a cream slice. 'I often thought I'd have been a whizz running one of those psychosexual clinics they're so bloody pretentious about nowadays.'

Ah, sure, wasn't it Frankie who had first told me that French kissing hadn't to be done in France and that the clitoris wasn't just a blob in Grey's *Anatomy*? And hadn't she been the one to pass around *The Perfumed Garden* at school and read Baudelaire at Vespers?

'But what'll Barney say?'

'Oh he'll rant and rave and call me everything under the sun but he'll come to terms with it. Has to. After all, his pension wouldn't keep us. And I'm not on the game or using Garland House as a knocking shop. No, Major B likes his cordon bleu cookery and his liqueur whisky and an extra two hundred pounds a month will let him have those.'

'But won't he feel a bit like a pimp?' I asked.

'Better a pimp than a pauper,' said the ever practical Frankie just as Coulter and Manners joined us.

Because I didn't want Frankie to start waving *Urge* at them as I knew she was very likely to do and because I still had Joan on my mind, I asked them all what they'd do about Joan Harris?

It was typical of me, Frankie said after she'd listened to my lack of success with Joan, it was typical of me to go worrying myself into a frazzle over a tiresome bitch of a girl who was intent on killing herself. Let her get on with it. The girl was right when she'd said that doctors had to lose their God-like image. We couldn't be expected to walk on water.

'You're right to call her bluff and let her home for the weekend,' Tony Manners said. 'And I bet anything you like she comes back. She's playing games with you. Needling you. Gives her a kick.'

'I'd give her a kick in the posterior,' said Coulter pompously. 'You shouldn't ever have taken her into hospital. If you treat patients like a Butlins Red Coat, roaring "Enjoy yourself damn you", then you're in for trouble. You offer her treatment, though whether any treatment will help this lass is dubious, and if she won't take it then that's it. Look, we only have so much oxygen and adrenalin and we have to spread them out so each patient gets his fair share.'

You had to be born with genes like Coulter's, I thought as I walked out after Frankie who accidently dropped *Urge* at the feet of an astounded looking senior male nurse. She picked it up and popped it in her bag with all the aplomb of a duchess who has dropped her satin drawers in Harrods.

9

One of my calls was to a bombed-out region which had been converted by the planners into a nightmare area, where enormously high towers reared up into the dirt-laden sky. Each building looked like a static rocket and each was exactly the same, the only differences were the pathetically grandiose names on the towers, 'Chatham House', 'Powerscourt House', 'Arden Court'. I drove through roads and roads flanked by the towering monstrous buildings. When I stopped to ask people where 'Elmhurst House' was, ten of them said they'd never heard of it although I found it three minutes later. The grass was faded, there were no flowers, and the inside of the high-rise building had the dreary concrete ugliness of a prison or a barracks. A kind fat woman struggling to reach one of the lift buttons told me to press on the other one.

'Odd numbers this side, that's me, and you want number one hundred and six, that's on the twelfth floor. Terrible these lifts. Half the time they don't work and the rest of the time they jam.'

Before I could risk her scorn and beg her to accompany me in my ascent she waddled into her lift and shot up leaving me to be jostled into the other lift by four West Indian lads in bobble caps and Bay City Roller pants. They looked as if they carried flick knives, but they were kind and gentle and courteously saw me up to the twelfth floor before they descended again to the fourth. All the doors were grim and uniform. There was no sound of children or music or cars, and I had a mad fancy that I was in a version of the Lubianka gaol.

The girl who answered my knock was young and pretty with a round face which still had the firm chubbiness of the teenager. She swung back her thick plait of brown hair, pulled up her jeans and asked me to follow her inside.

The flat itself was big and airy and bright, but there was the oppressive quiet, although the fat gurgling baby in the play-pen made his own bubbling song and the girl switched off the TV.

'I keep it on all the time Jake's gone to work,' she said. 'It's more company than the radio.'

I could see she had been crying and her eyes were desperate. When she picked up the baby, who had begun to howl, her own tears dripped down and mixed with her son's.

'What's the matter, love? I don't know your name,' I said.

Well I did have her name written down on Mrs Bell's list but I didn't want to go scrambling for it.

'It's Diane,' she said. 'Diane Fentham.'

She walked up and down patting the crying child gently until it stopped wailing and began to burble happily again.

'Wind,' she said, setting him back in his play-pen.

'Or maybe he senses you're unhappy,' I said. That did it. Her mouth opened like a child who's been slapped and she sobbed.

'I shouldn't be. I've got everything. Jake, me husband, is marvellous to me. And Perry . . .' she pointed to the play-pen, 'he's a darling. But I . . . I . . .' She began to sob again, and because she'd used all her paper hankies I handed her some of my own.

'It's just that I hate these flats. I hate 'em. I come from a place, well it's not the country but there's green, and the people in the shops know you and you can go out for walks and things, but here, I can't describe it. I can't really. The flat itself's all right. . . .'

It was. The rooms were large and spacious, the carpeting was soft and wall-to-wall and the furniture was starkly modern but comfortable. There was an enormous TV and intricate and expensive hi-fi equipment in one corner. But the quiet hung down on us like an oppressive entity and there was nothing to see or hear which reminded you that you were in touch with humanity.

'I'd rather live in a grotty street where there was people passing and kids playing and . . . and . . .'

She burst into more tears, her face swollen and blotched. It was all right for her husband, he went out to work, she continued, and when he told her to make friends with the other women in the high-rise tower she couldn't make him see that there was no one to make friends with because most of the women who were able to went out to work or else were too old. The girls with children in the same position as herself were just as miserable, all of them on tranquillizers and two of them had tried overdoses.

'One girl flung herself off the balcony last year,' Diane said. 'Shocking, isn't it? And yet . . . yet sitting here sometimes, looking out, wishing I could look out on a street and see people passing, I can understand it. What the girl did, I mean. Doctor Potts is giving me these for depression.'

She pulled out a bottle of yellow anti-depressant tablets. Yes, she was depressed. What she needed was company, the contact with other humans. Her diagnosis was loneliness.

'Would you like a cup of tea?'

I didn't want one. I had my other calls to make, but her need to talk to someone was so great that I hadn't the heart to say 'No'.

A few minutes later she brought in tea and after glancing at Perry, who was curled up asleep with his limbs hanging limply and his thumb stuffed in his mouth, she said, handing me a mug of tea, 'Mum can't understand it. Me being like this. She says she had to bring up five kids in a house with rats in the back yard, no indoor toilet and there was never enough money for her to be sure of the rent and food and clothes. But we was happy. We used to have a right giggle . . . nobody laughs here . . . nobody looks at you or says Hallo.'

Maybe they were all feeling miserable too, I suggested, and thanked her for the tea and said that I'd write to Doctor Potts.

'It sounds awful,' Diane said at the door. The cold landing was silent and still. 'It sounds awful, but I can't wait for Perry to be older so I can get out and get a job. Not for the money, but for the company.'

Poor Diane, I thought driving on to my next port of call. Wasn't her reaction entirely natural to her circumstances, and wouldn't I feel just as desperate in her situation?

My next patient, Peter Ridley, lived in Tanners Lane which was a maddening place to find because the road sign was defaced and the lane was situated well behind a row of houses which looked as if they were awaiting the bulldozer. The man who answered the bell of No 89 was crackling with an abnormal animation. He was small and slender, with glaring hazel eyes and a shock of dark hair which he pushed back from his pale face with long nicotine-stained fingers.

I realized that Doctor Porter, a woman GP whose judgment on her patients was very sound, was again proved right. 'Watch it,' she had said, 'Mr Ridley will keep you for hours if you let him. It's not that he won't tell you about his problems, he'll tell you too much.'

Mr Ridley asked me to sit down, and waving his arms around the cluttered room, begged me to excuse the untidiness. The room was like the office of a solicitor who had gone berserk. Law books were piled and stacked everywhere, the floor and tables were littered with legal documents and the mantelpiece was piled with stacks of letters and cards.

'It's hard to know where to start,' said Mr Ridley, lighting a cigarette. How thin he was, I noticed, and the baggy old pullover had more holes than wool in it.

'I'm a chemist, a biochemist,' he began, and I knew that was true because Dr Porter had told me. 'But I got a bit bored with the scientific life so I bought a fish and chip shop. . . .'

Surely an odd thing to do? Not at all, Mr Ridley went on; it didn't make money of course, he explained, and described the circumstances of why it didn't with such fluent articulateness that I nearly had to wave my watch in his face to get him moving with his history.

His wife and he had been happy enough, he said, until a lay preacher had winkled his way into her affections and she had run off with this man who was called Cornelius Hammer.

I asked Mr Ridley to repeat the name, it sounded as bizarre as those you found in American novels. Indeed, Mr Ridley's story ran like a novel. His wife had decamped with Mr Hammer, the children and all the cash, leaving Mr Ridley with a bankrupt business, no job and a burning desire to punish Mr Hammer. He had been unable to get his wife back, Mr Ridley went on, but he was involved at the moment in four law suits, three connected with Mr Hammer, and one with a fraud perpetrated on him by his employers in a temporary job with an industrial concern.

'I could take a degree in law now,' Mr Ridley waved his cigarette at all the books and documents. 'I know the British legal system backwards. I could quote you cases for the next three hours, and as for the way the courts and judiciary operate, well. . . .'

Mr Ridley gave a cynical smile and launched once again into the saga of his troubles. I believe the substance of his extraordinary story was true, but the man himself, if not unbalanced, was certainly not quite sane. Why set out on such a doomed gesture as buying a fish and chip shop when he had an honours science degree? And why did his wife really run off? And why did he think he could deal with all these intricate and complicated cases without a solicitor at least?

What to do about the paranoid and over-active Mr Ridley? He looked ill and undernourished and his eyes burned with such fanaticism that, when after an inescapable two hours I could get a break in his flow of talk, I suggested his coming into hospital for a rest. He said adamantly that was quite impossible. He had to be here to deal with the immense flow of letters that kept arriving. Dr Porter had given him tranquillizers, he went on, kindly meant no doubt, but didn't we both realize that he had to keep his brain unfogged to be able to write replies to the mass of letters and have his wits about him to make his case?

I looked around the bleak little room, cold because there was only a heater with one bar, and compared it to the warm comfort of Diane's high-rise flat. I had a mental vision of poor Mr Ridley sitting in his worn pullover, sustained by coffee and cigarettes, writing letters all through the night. He looked as if he could do with twenty-four hours' sleep.

He was intelligent. His dark eyes had the fervour of an old-time preacher as he described in suffocating detail, for the second time, all his various legal battles, sueing Mr Hammer, trying to get custody of his children and bringing his employers to justice over the money they owed him. Oh yes, he was bright; lack of brains wasn't his trouble. But emotionally he was sick, paranoid and hypomanic, yet not mad enough to have treatment forced on him. We could only wait and see.

Like Diane, Mr Ridley wanted me to stay and hear him out, but it was after five o'clock, the traffic was getting bad and I had to reach No. 105 Gladstone Street, Godley.

I found the district, and indeed the street, after a long and tiring drive, but half the numbers in the two shabby rows were of houses which had been pulled down, or where this hadn't happened they had been made invisible by peeling paint. In the end I asked a hatchet-faced woman with a turban if she knew where No. 105 was?

'Over there.' She pointed to a dilapidated house opposite. 'Going to see young Jackie Printer are you? He's a nutter if ever I saw one. Going round like a rasher of bacon saying "Peace". Listen, are you a doctor?'

I foolishly said I was and she said she thought so, and after seeing the Printer lad she'd be glad if I'd call and have a word with her.

'It's these turns I get,' she said. 'I go all dizzy and hot and cold and then I starts to shake and. . . .'

It was after six o'clock and tiredness made me ruthless. She'd better see her own doctor, I said, I really couldn't interfere with a colleague's patients.

'I have,' she yelled, as I crossed the road to the Printer house. 'I have seen him. He's a coloured chap and he don't give a God damn. "It's your age," that's all he says.'

The man who answered my knock was Mr Printer, senior. A small precise man who looked what he was, a clerk.

'In here, Doctor. I'll just get Jackie,' he said. 'I'm afraid Mrs Printer is busy giving the children their tea. Poor Jackie's been very odd for weeks now. He lives on fruit juice, won't eat at all and just sits smiling and staring into space. I think he needs a tonic or something.'

Jackie needed far more than a tonic, I decided, when the gentle eighteen-year-old drifted in, smiling the absorbed smile of the schizophrenic, to whom reality has become distorted and terrifying, and only to be dealt with by extraordinary means as he was doing now. Jesus had told him not to eat so 'Peace would come to the world', he told me, and so he must obey Him.

Jackie was a handsome boy with a mop of rolling curls hanging on thin shoulders. His jeans and sweat shirt hung loosely on his emaciated body. 'Peace' was printed on the tee shirt which hung on his hollow chest.

'Just going through a phase, isn't he?' Remarkable how even a normally intelligent man like Mr Printer couldn't see how mad his son was. But who wanted to admit that their child was crazy?

'Are the voices talking to you all the time, Jackie?' I asked.

He smiled, that slow secret smile, and said no, not at all times, but only to remind him to take nothing but fruit juice.

What if he died, I asked, and he said, well if God called him then he was prepared to go.

Jackie got up, went to the window and made a sudden gesture, flinging his skinny arms wide in a sacrificial way and mouthing silently to the passers-by.

That's the way he was all the time, his father said, either sitting in his room or else going to the window or the street and telling people not to eat and make peace.

'I suppose they think the lad's bonkers,' Mr Printer said, 'but I think he may need a bit of help, Doctor.'

I told Mr Printer as gently as possible that his son was very ill. I didn't go into why he was ill, glad that Mr Printer was satisfied with the diagnosis of a 'phase', for the moment anyway.

Jackie received the news that he was to go into hospital with a bland lack of interest.

'As long as they don't make me eat,' he said. 'Jesus doesn't want that. . . .'

'Well, there'll be fruit juice,' I temporized, and told Mr Printer to bring his son to Barrington Hall that very evening.

As I was going through the gate the woman who got the 'turns' pounced on me again.

'I've been down to that doctor again,' she said, 'and he said it was all in me mind and I should lose weight. What does he think I am? A nutter like Jackie Printer or something. I gave him a piece of me mind I can tell you, and do you know, the nasty bugger told me I wouldn't speak to him like that if he was white. . . .'

Fortunately a lorry passed, making such a rattling din that I was able to make my escape, no doubt giving the woman another of her 'turns'.

10

Joan Harris went out for a day in care of her husband. In spite of
Frankie's, Manners's and Coulter's down-to-earth advice to quit
worrying and let the girl make her own choice between life and
death I couldn't stop myself ringing the ward on the evening of
her return to ask whether all was well. Logan was off duty but an
efficient young West Indian nurse called Sister Pearl assured me
that Joan had returned, looking as calm as usual and was now on
her way to bed. I felt relieved and even a bit hopeful. Maybe, just
maybe, she was going to try and keep her options open on life.

Next day I was on duty for twenty-four hours and I was called
to St Peter's where a group of young people who'd had a drug
party and were all suffering the effects of a bad trip were making
a rumpus in Casualty. I discharged the pot smokers and sent two
young men who had well and truly freaked out up to Barrington
Hall and then decided to call and see Dr Jack Duggan who was
still a patient in St Peter's after his heart attack. 'It must be the
Librium he's on,' the pert young nurse who showed me where his
room was remarked. 'Dr Williams has told him he must rest, but
that doesn't stop him groping.'

I nearly said that that wasn't the Librium but Duggan's
randiness. However, some vestige of professional loyalty stopped
me and I tapped on Jack's door. There was a scraping sound and
when I entered the room a full-blown lady whom Jack introduced as Mrs Compton, his housekeeper, was rearranging her
blouse over an ample bosom.

'Well, you're looking well,' I said falsely. His colour was a
nasty shade of purple and his breath came in rasping pants.

'And I feel marvellous. All due, of course, to Mrs Compton
here who fortunately happened to find me flaked out at three in
the morning.'

Mrs Compton bridled and murmured something about having to go, but Jack slapped her fat hand affectionately and said not at all, not at all. How were things at the hospital, he asked.

'Oh fine,' I said. 'Fine. I'm enjoying it, doing the visits and that. It's very interesting.'

As soon as I said it I realized it was the wrong thing. In spite of his seedy life and the medical whoppers he was constantly making, Jack regarded himself as the Senior Consultant at Barrington Hall and now he trumpeted like an old seal in danger of losing his territory.

'Do you indeed?' he sniffed. 'Well, you'll soon find out that it's not all chat and chuckles.' Then he added coldly, 'Sorry I can't offer you a drink. Not allowed the stuff.'

That was a lie because I could see the two empty glasses and smelt the whisky. Jack might have been forbidden alcohol but rules never bothered him. He began to pat Mrs Compton's plump hands again and stared at the window. It seemed to be getting darker, he remarked, and the weather forecast was bad. I knew I was being dismissed.

As I said my goodbyes he pulled himself up on his pillows. 'Williams assures me,' he declared, 'that I'll be back in a couple of weeks. Won't be long passing. Thanks for coming. Frankie looked in yesterday. What the hell does she see in that old man she lives with? Has he got money or what? Fine-looking woman, she could do better for herself. Must be money. Couldn't be anything else.'

I wasn't prepared to be probed about Frankie. Jack ought to have known that, because Frankie's affair with Barney was a continual source of lewd interest to him and I'd parried his attempts to pump me about the pair on many occasions. He crudely divided women into two categories, bedworthy or not-bedworthy, and Frankie definitely came into the former group; it was incomprehensible to his limited imagination that a woman of Frankie's still-nubile charms should be bound to an old has-been like Barney unless Barney made it worth her while with money.

Jack Duggan could have had a psychic flash in saying that I'd find life wasn't all 'chat and chuckles' because when I got back to my house and was just finishing my supper the phone went. It was Sister Pearl to say that Joan Harris had swallowed an overdose. She had been washed out and treated at St Peter's and was now back in Parker ward.

Blast and double blast. Just as I was thinking there might be a chance for her. And why had she taken the tablets in the ward and not when she was out on leave? She must have brought them in hidden in her purse. What was going to happen to her? We couldn't keep pumping her out and reviving her. The next time would be the third time and maybe that would be the fatal one that she'd consider lucky.

'Why, Joan?' I asked. She was lying in a side room, her face as white as her hospital robe, and her hair hung damp and stringy around her hollowed face. The disconcerting eyes were sunken and glazed and her lips were colourless.

'I told you. I keep telling you. I don't want to live. I tried the tablets you ordered and they don't do me no good. Nothing does. I've bloody botched things again.'

'Why did you tell the nurses that you'd swallowed the tablets? Wasn't that more than botching it? Wasn't it more a cry for help?'

The slanted almost lashless eyes avoided mine and she turned away and stared mutely out of the window. It was nearly October and the rain made a steady drumming against the dark window.

'You're wasting your time,' she said. 'Why don't you give it to those that need it? I'm not mad. And I can't help being the way I am.'

'Can't you give life a chance?' I asked. 'You're young enough for the possibility of life changing for you and making you want to live.'

'I've given it over five years now and it doesn't get any better. It gets worse.'

I had never felt so hopelessly impotent with any other patient. Frankie and the others were right. This girl couldn't be saved. She was lost, doomed by her own profound melancholia. Only a miracle such as some profound religious experience could save her and for her, as for many young people I saw, God was dead.

I felt sodden and sad myself as I left her room and went down the corridor towards the front entrance. A thin figure dressed in a scruffy black suit was coming out of the main ward. It was Father Mortimer the RC chaplain.

Mortimer was in his forties but with his cadaverous face and thin straggles of hair he looked much older. Because he worked far too hard at his busy parish in Rigton, suffered from a serious heart condition and wasn't looked after by his housekeeper he always appeared as if he needed an immediate transfusion, but any attempts to move him to a quieter parish met with his stern opposition. If he made me think of Bertie Wooster, there was nothing Woosterish about his mind which was clear and sharp. That, along with a will of iron, made him a good and well-respected priest. In spite of the fact that he was ruthless about using anyone he thought could help him with the crowd of sad humanity that he collected, I had a lot of time for Mortimer. He didn't preach. He practised.

I decided to talk to him about Joan and he said, looking at his watch, that yes, he had time before Benediction and anyway he wanted to speak to *me* about something.

Over tea, brought to us by a student nurse, I poured out my concern about Joan. Nobody or nothing seemed to help her and I wondered if he would have a word with her?

'I assume she's agreeable?' he asked gently. 'One can't ram the Almighty down people's throats, Doctor.'

'I know,' I said. 'She's not a Catholic. She's nothing and she wants to return to nothing.

'Then that's really her business, isn't it?' he said. I was surprised. His realism shocked me. 'Are you sure it isn't your own *pride* at your apparent lack of ability to help her that's worrying you?'

Maybe that was true but anyway I'd ask her whether she would see him, I said.

'If she agrees, then I will. Not otherwise,' he said.

I slipped back into Joan's room. She was still lying quite still staring out of the window, her supper on the tray beside her bed untouched.

Would she be agreeable to seeing the hospital chaplain, I asked her? He was a nice person and a good man and maybe she could talk to him better than to me?

'You don't give up, do you?' Her voice was hoarse because of the tube that had been thrust down her throat during the wash out.

'I don't believe in a God. Even if I thought there was one I wouldn't want to know Him. I won't see anyone. I just want to be left alone.'

It was no good, I told Father, and he said that he'd expected as much. You couldn't force Faith on people. Trying to divert me, he told me he'd been seeing a young Catholic girl who was due to have a termination. She was three months pregnant and although she was determined to have the abortion she had asked to see him because she wanted him to understand. Her Catholicism had filled her with guilt so she tried to justify her decision.

'So I had to tell her she couldn't have an abortion and a blessing,' Mortimer said.

'Now', he went on, 'you look tired, Doctor, and I hate to be holding you up but I wanted to discuss my new curate with you. I'm terribly worried about him. You know Father Mason, do you?'

Yes, I did. Father Mike Mason had caused quite a stir when he'd joined the parish a few months ago. He'd got a first at Oxford and become a convert to Catholicism, with what according to Mortimer was undue haste. It wasn't just his cerebral powers that made him outstanding but his dazzling good looks. What with his lambent hazel eyes and flowing golden hair plus the artiness of his non-clerical dress he made a dazzling contrast with Mortimer and Father Mulligan, the other curate, who was a publican's son and spoke with a Bootle accent. Mason had started all sorts of new projects and schemes and was just back from taking a crowd of youths to Russia. He had marched in Ban the Bomb processions and had headed a few demos.

'Just takes off on that beastly motor bike and one doesn't know where he's off to,' Father Mortimer continued. 'He dines out several times a week with what passes for the local gentry and he patronizes poor Father Mulligan terribly. I wouldn't mind but his mother's a dear little soul. She says her son was quite all right until he went to Oxford.'

Father Mortimer blew his nose with a handkerchief which had obviously never experienced an iron. I was tired and cold and hungry and I wished he'd get to the point. So curates these days were uncertain, always leaping over the wall and into matrimony as if, Father Mortimer had said once, 'as if the marriage state was the secret of eternal bliss.' And there had been the curate before Mason who had got a barmaid pregnant. Well, it wasn't women this time, Father went on. In his opinion Father Mason was a homosexual and a practising one at that. Last Sunday at High Mass he'd been struck by the fact that Father Mason's hair was more golden than usual and he was convinced that the hue had come out of a bottle.

'And he was ogling, actually ogling, one of the altar boys. It's most worrying. What can I do, doctor?'

'Nothing much at the moment,' I said. 'You'd have to catch him *in flagrante* as it were.'

'So distressing.' Father looked transparently pallid and the veins on his forehead were throbbing alarmingly. 'Father Moran can't stand him, you know.'

Moran was a lumbering priest from County Clare whose shaky theology and rubrics were made up for by the loving care with which he'd built up the other parish in Rigton.

'I shall have to have a chat with the Abbot,' Father Mortimer said, heaving himself to his feet, his arthritic joints creaking like castanets.

Yes, yes, I said, that was the thing to do. I'd met the Abbot once and he'd struck me as being a most sensible and balanced man with the right amount of sophistication mixed with piety.

'It seems that sex is the new religion,' Father remarked as we walked towards the front. 'I shall have to do something about it.'

I didn't quite know what he meant by that but there was no doubt about the Freudian association of ideas when, on the way to his old banger of a car, he asked how Frances was getting on? For an awful moment I wondered whether he'd heard about her assignment on *Urge*, but then I dismissed the idea. Frankie could be secretive enough when she chose and she'd given up practising Catholicism a long time ago.

Because Father Mortimer had old-fashioned and Puritanical ideas about sex I knew he disapproved of her association with Barney, but because he also had a large, generous and charitable heart he didn't allow his disapproval of her life style to interfere with his liking for her as a person. And she'd helped too many of his parishioners for him to be petty about her fleshly sins.

'I think he sees me as a sort of latter-day Mary Magdalen,' Frankie had told me. 'The role rather appeals to my sense of drama!'

'Yes indeed. Sex is in and death is out,' Father said as he opened his car. 'You can say what you like about sex but you mustn't mention dying or growing old. It's the children I worry about. I must do something. The Lord will guide me in the right direction.'

With a series of lurches and chugging noises he shot off in his wheezing car.

11

Joan Harris became stronger physically if not emotionally, but there were no more attempts at suicide. She seemed to be making a slight but definite effort to co-operate and went home for three week-ends without incident. I had as a precaution contacted a very competent social worker called Mr Paley who arranged for her children to be taken into care. Both of us agreed that the elder child in particular was in danger and Mr Harris was so inadequate that he still referred to his wife's suicide attempts as 'moods' and just an indication of the mysteries of the female psyche.

I had thought that Joan would have been bitter at her children being removed from her but she didn't say much, beyond a laconic, 'They'll be better off. They're always all right when they're away from me.'

It occurred to me that she might possibly feel relieved at not having to cope with them, or even see their absence as the green light to go ahead and do away with herself. After a few weeks she asked to see me and I was surprised to find how well she looked. Make-up and good food improved her so much that I realized that she seemed quite a pretty girl. Her unusual eyes would have been beautiful except for their penetrating stare. She had something to ask me, she said. Would I please allow her to be discharged? Her section had only a few days to run anyway.

I had no real grounds for keeping her. She wasn't mentally disturbed within the meaning of the Mental Health Act. The fact that she wanted to die could be construed as a personality disorder or a basic human right according to your psychiatric orientation. I couldn't do any more for her except agree to let her go. But the niggling sense of duty towards her made me ask whether she would accept psychotherapy at a nearby clinic which specialized in treating personality disorders.

'I've heard about that dump,' she said in her flat monotonous voice. 'I'm not going there. Just to listen to a crowd of old women gabbing.'

'They're not old folk and they don't spend their time gabbing,' I said, feeling the usual annoyance that she always roused in me.

'I'll come to your out-patients,' she said. I was so surprised that my face must have shown it because she gave a frosty smile and said, 'That shook you!'

'Look, Joan,' I said, 'I'm too long in the tooth and too busy for playing games and you're playing one with me. If I agree to see you at my out-patients in St Peter's will you give me an undertaking that you won't do away with yourself till you see me? Or give me due warning that you intend to do so.'

She actually laughed. It was more of a croak but it was something. Even though she was playing games, Russian roulette with her life, it was some infinitesimal advance that she was now able to show some emotion other than self hatred.

'I can't promise but I'll try,' she said.

'A rum girl,' observed Logan when Joan had gone out. 'But I agree with you; there's nothing more we can do except let her go.'

'It is, I suppose, what the text books would describe as "an intractable depression",' Lia Gupta said, when I called in her office. 'I don't suppose she'll turn up to see you at the out-patients.'

'I don't know,' I answered, 'I really don't know. But it's odd that although she's not a dim girl, she never yet has succeeded in killing herself, isn't it?'

My musings were interrupted by a phone call to say that Mr Ignatius O'Halloran had arrived last night very drunk and complaining of feeling depressed.

'Not half as depressed as I am to hear he's back,' I told the young male nurse. 'I'll be over to see him.'

O'Halloran was unshaven and shaky and so full of grovelling apology that I had to prise myself loose from him when he threw himself on the floor and grabbed my waist. Squashed into a hospital dressing-gown which was too tight, he tried to assemble his twitching limbs and he was having difficulty with his swollen tongue which seemed to be stuck to the floor of his mouth.

'I've no excuse, no excuse, doctor.' O'Halloran cast wild and anguished eyes at the ceiling. 'I must have had a hurricane to the brain or something. The wife's people moved in with us, you see. The only bit of peace I could get was in the pub and now the wife's gone off back to Ireland with the children leaving me on me own.'

Maudlin tears filled his bloodshot eyes and he rummaged shakily at an empty packet of cigarettes.

I had a notion to turn him over to the cold clinical assessment of Coulter but I knew that after one raking glance Coulter would throw him out. Let's face it, he hadn't got to where he was by being kind to hopeless soaks like O'Halloran.

'OK. We'll detoxicate you, Mr O'Halloran,' I said.

O'Halloran rallied his remaining cerebral resources and asked what 'detoxicating' meant? I explained that he'd need drugs and injections to combat the poisonous effects of the alcohol, after which he'd stop trembling and sweating.

'And then, Mr O'Halloran, then it's up to you. Any more drinking here and you're out, never to come back.'

'I'll get down on me knees and promise. I'll get on me knees and swear by me dead mother . . .'

Before any such embarrassing enactions could occur I signalled to the nurse to help the shaking, shuffling O'Halloran out and back to bed where he was to start his course of concentrated vitamin injections.

'There's a man been admitted during the night, doctor,' the nurse said urgently when she reached me. 'His name is Joseph Ingham and he's been talking and acting in a peculiar way.'

'Show him in,' I said as she led O'Halloran away.

The first impression of Ingham was his bulk. He was a broad bull-like man with a brick-red face and a thick mop of very curly black hair. When he was young he must have been handsome in an Italianate sort of way.

'Mind if I smoke?' His hands were enormously muscular, like the rest of him.

68

'I hear you've been having some trouble, Mr Ingham,' I said. 'Would you like to tell me about it?'

'Well, it's these voices I keep hearing like. I get 'em bad all the time but they're worse when I've had a drink.'

'What do they say to you?'

'Things like "Get the bastard" and "Do for him".'

'Do those remarks refer to anyone that you know?'

'Too right. It's that Charlie Hazel.'

Gradually, with much prompting because the Ingham brain didn't move fast, I got the story. He had worked on a building site with a Charlie Hazel who had been in the habit of nicking things. When this was discovered Hazel involved Ingham who had been sent down for two years on Hazel's evidence.

'And I'll get him for it. I'll get him.'

'But you may be up on a murder charge yourself?'

'I don't care. I'll swing for that Hazel bastard. I'm always ready for him, see. I carry an axe.'

'You what?'

'I carry an axe. Oh I didn't bring it in here with me but I take it when I go out in the evenings.'

This sounded very nasty. The only thing that was odd was that although he'd been carrying the axe for four years now he still hadn't used it. But maybe he hadn't met up with Hazel yet.

'I'll find the sod one of these nights,' Ingham said, twisting his ham-like hands. 'I go round the pubs, you know, doing a bit of singing.'

When he went out young Nurse Yates told me that this was indeed true and that she'd heard Ingham in The Yellow Man only last week.

'His favourite song is "I did it my way",' Yates added.

Well I'd better do things my way too, I decided and I rang the local police. I hated doing this and it was only the second time I'd ever reported a patient to the police in all my career, but I didn't like this talk of an axe and the paranoid determination of Ingham.

'Oh yes. We know that bloke,' said Detective-Sergeant Mills. 'He's known locally as "The Hatchet Man". Frequents The Yellow Man, doesn't he?'

'That's right,' I said. 'I think he's very disturbed mentally but he talks of voices telling him to murder this man Hazel and says that he always carries this axe when he goes out.'

'Well, no one's actually seen it but we keep an eye on him just the same. There's been a few murders in the last year where no arrest was made and they were all in the vicinity of The Yellow Man. You'll let us know if Ingham goes out or is discharged, will you, Doctor?'

I said I would and added that as I lived on my own I didn't want Ingham to get to know anything about my ringing the police. Of course, of course, Mills said soothingly. And if he or his lads wanted to come up to the hospital it would only be with my permission and they would of course wear plain clothes.

*   *   *

I was just finishing my clinic that afternoon when the phone went and it was Father Mortimer. He had a little favour to ask me he said. My heart did a nose dive. Father's favours always involved drunken layabouts, battered wives or husbands and the human wreckage who kept up a continual barrage on the door of his tumble-down parochial house. No wonder Mrs Butterley, his housekeeper, had so many 'funny turns', I often thought.

'I've been thinking of the conversation we had, doctor. How is that girl, by the way?'

This was for openers, so I said I was discharging her and it was over to the Lord.

'He won't let her down,' Father said. His view of the Almighty was that of a kindly and jolly old man who'd be too much of a decent chap to let anyone go to Hell. Frankie said that Mortimer's God was not the terrifying Jehovah-like figure of our Irish Catholicism but more of a benevolent Santa Claus with presents for all, albeit that the delivery might be late.

'Well, you'll have heard of our Catholic Marriage Guidance Clinic, held monthly?'

I had. I'd heard about it from many of the Catholic GPs who'd been roped in to assist in explaining the Catholic views on marriage and the rhythm method of contraception to the parishioners, mostly female, who cared to attend.

'It's a farce,' Dr Peggy Malloy had told me. 'Like folk having their diet and then demanding their dinner, the women that come are nearly all on the Pill but think if they use the Rhythm Method as well that that'll square things with God. And it's murder trying to instruct them in the taking of their rectal temperature. As one woman said, how can she have a steady hand to insert the thermometer up her rectum when the baby is crying and her family are waiting for their supper?'

And I'd seen the room where the clinics were conducted. The walls were festooned with huge pictures of the itinerary of the ovum as it travelled from huge unlikely looking wombs along tubes which looked like worms having convulsions. Poor Father was so gratified at even getting a sprinkling of attendances that nobody had the heart to tell him that most of the women were also attending the Family Planning Association up the road to get fixed up with loops and coils as well as supplies of the Pill.

For an awful moment I thought he was going to ask me to give a session to the Marriage Guidance Clinic, especially as I knew that fond as the local Catholic doctors were of the priest, they'd almost all dropped out of doing the clinics except for Peggy and a few stalwart practitioners like her. But no, what he wanted of me was worse.

He was appalled, he said, by the ignorance of the facts of life shown by the ten and eleven-year-olds attending St Bede's, the parish school, and he proposed to form a panel to give the children's parents some guidance on how to attend to their duties in informing their offspring about sexual matters. There would be Mr Vickers the headmaster, himself, Mrs Massey, a teacher, and, he hoped, myself.

Oh I couldn't, I really couldn't, I told him. That sort of thing wasn't in my line at all. I was dying to suggest the obvious person, Frankie, and when Father paused I said that Frankie had vast experience of general practice and moreover she actually liked public speaking. She lectured to the student nurses, I went on, and everyone said how well she managed to put things over. Surely she was the one to ask?

'I think not,' said Father and I knew that there was no use

71

asking him why. I suspected it was because he couldn't condone her ménage with Barney. To Father that was still living in sin and as such a bad example to youth. No, he said, he was sure I'd do it awfully well. The meeting was to be held at the school on next Wednesday evening at seven o'clock.

'But I'm not really in touch with young people,' I said desperately. 'I don't know how much they know or how much they ought to know. Or how to tell them.'

'It's not so much the children as the parents,' Father said. 'If the parents know their facts then it will be easier for them to tell their children. I'm sure you'll make an excellent job of it, Doctor.'

There was no escape. Father Mortimer had a knack of getting his own way.

'Our poor children are so exposed to the sordid stream of filth in books, magazines and the media,' he went on. 'Could you get over to the parents that they must tell their children in a sensitive, civilized way? I do dislike all this use of anatomical jargon that you doctors have started. Wouldn't it be nicer to call the penis a "tassel" or something, and instead of saying "semen" you could mention "the seed of love"?'

I had a wild impulse to burst out laughing. Poor Father was so upper-class and patrician that much as he loved his parishioners he'd never really understand their robust earthiness. I dreaded having to come out with things like 'the seed of love' to the Rigtonians but there was no escape from the lecture.

'I'm not sure, Father,' I tried a last ditch attempt at reneging, 'I don't know that I believe in sex instruction, not like this. I don't think I'm properly motivated.'

'Never mind the motivation. Just get out there and do it,' said Father with one of his surprising changes to a rather martial tone of command.

12

I couldn't wait to see Frankie. I wanted to tell her about my awful assignment at St Bede's and also to know how she was getting on with her work for the porno magazine. I'd only encountered her once in the last few weeks and then she was pounding up the corridor of the hospital carrying a bulging briefcase and a pile of books. The magazine was sending her the readers' letters direct to the house, she told me.

'And I'm not kidding, Joyce; they're dynamite. I never realized people's sex lives were so complicated. I had a letter this morning from a girl who's engaged but says she'd rather sleep with her Alsatian. Barney says I should tell her to look for a man who says "Woof".'

'How's Barney taking it?'

'Oh, grumbling as usual. He's been seeing a lot of old Sullivan and tippling so much that his bloody gout has flared up which makes him as irritable as a bag of weasels.'

I wasn't surprised. Old Sullivan was a withered-looking skeleton of a man who shared Barney's nostalgic memories of India under the Raj and agreed that the only way to combat the miseries of modern life in an Empireless Britain was to use the anaesthesia of whisky.

When I went over to Garland House that night Frankie answered the door with her blouse on back to front and her hair sticking out from its straggling bun. The sitting room was in a shambles, toppling piles of papers and letters lay beside the typewriter on the writing table, Willy the dog barked crossly at me from behind the sofa and when I sat down I felt something hard under me. It was an enormous black bra which Frankie snatched from me and threw over a black dressmaker's dummy standing in a corner.

'Christ, I've hardly had time to go to the lavatory,' she said, pouring two massive glasses of wine. 'What with doing surgeries for Cousins, getting through the hospital work and dealing with these.' She pointed to the pile of letters on the table. 'Every day they come pouring in. I'm beginning to dread the postman. This is the sort of stuff . . .'

She passed me a sheaf of letters and a brief glance at the contents was enough for me. They were sad and funny and made me realize that there were even lonelier people in the world than those who came to my clinics.

'I am a bank clerk with a compulsion to wear ladies' knickers. As I suffer from diabetes I'm afraid of passing out, when my secret will be discovered.'

'I am male except in anatomy. I will pay anything to have my breasts removed. Please can you give me the address of a surgeon willing to do this? Otherwise I will kill myself.'

'My wife and I both suffer from multiple sclerosis but we both desire to have sex and we are too shy to ask anyone. They never mention it at the hospital and we think that maybe it will be dangerous for us to indulge even if we knew how.'

I couldn't read any more. The desperation of the writers leaped out of the pages and clawed at my heart. I told Frankie so and she nodded. 'It's why people write to the backs of women's magazines and lady columnists on newspapers. People trust them more than doctors, who always seem too remote and too hurried to listen. It's a failure of the medical profession.'

I told her about Father Mortimer roping me in to speak to parents about sex instruction, and she said comfortably that that would be a doddle. Yes, I said, compared to her chore in answering the *Urge* queries, of course it would, but didn't she agree that although everyone was now far more sophisticated about sex than ten years ago, poor Father Mortimer was still too rarefied about things?

'Sure. That's why he has such trouble with those young swingers he gets as curates. Have you seen the new raver, Mason? I believe he's a member of Gay Lib.'

'I bet Father M still thinks "gay" means joyous,' I said.

Willy shook himself and lumbered towards the door barking

expectantly.

'That'll be Barney,' Frankie said. 'He says his hearing has gone completely today but he's heard you and you know how he hates to be left out of things. What with me being too busy to give him all the attention he thinks he should get and his toes giving him gyp he's as sour as be damned.'

That was an understatement. Barney came in looking thunderous. In spite of his gout and ill-temper he was as usual immaculately dressed in a dark blue dressing-gown with a maroon cravat. White hair carefully arranged, clear eyes and smooth roseate skin indicated rest and a careful toilet. He smelled of pine essence.

'One gets very tired of being ignored,' he said, helping himself to a drink. 'I'm to be denied sustenance as well as company now, am I?'

'If sustenance means booze then you know what Cousins told you,' Frankie said. 'Gout and whisky don't go together.'

'Spare me unsolicited medical advice.'

Barney drew a hand over his rubicund face. He had decided on martyred tactics, I could see. I'd bet he'd rehearsed his attitude in the bathroom. I often thought what a marvellous actor he'd have made in the old barn-storming days.

'I am surrounded by letters from maniacs who haven't the decency to learn to live with their ghastly private lives. Such hearing as I have left is being destroyed by the battering of Frankie's typewriter, giving of her wisdom to these lunatics, and when I *do* manage to get out to spend some time with an old friend who has similar interests to myself I am castigated next day by a woman who professes to have a regard for me.'

'Now listen mate . . .'

'Please, please, leave that sort of language to the degenerate young louts who read *Urge*,' Barney sighed.

'I don't object to your going out to meet Jeremiah Sullivan at all. I wish you'd go out more. But just because the two of you got sloshed don't blame me for your hangover,' Frankie flared.

'"Hangover," did she say "hangover"?' Barney asked me, professing not to have heard.

'Yes. You fell over a chair last night and told me there were

75

burglars in the house. You saw your own muddy footsteps and kept yelling that we'd been burgled. I had to slip you two sleeping pills instead of one,' Frankie said. 'What vicious lies,' Barney said with dignity. 'I did no such thing. The trouble with you is that you've taken on too much with this sordid job. Yes, sordid for a professional person. Although I suppose it must give you a vicarious satisfaction to read such filthy letters. You don't get it from me, isn't that it? Oh, I know, I know. Naturally, you want a younger man. You're a normal healthy woman. You have urges. I can't satisfy them. So I'm to be treated with pity. Kept warm, fed, allowed the odd treat. Willy has a better life than me. If you had any love for me at all you'd give me more than two pills and let me get out of this bloody awful hell I'm going through.'

There were tears in Barney's eyes and if I hadn't heard him like this before I'd have almost died of pity and embarrassment. But I knew he was just abreacting, goading Frankie into a response which would complete his catharsis.

'No wonder your wife left you, you self-pitying old bugger,' Frankie said. 'No one could call you a dirty old man but by Christ you're a nasty old man.'

'I can't hear you. I've gone completely deaf. And my eyes hurt. Maybe I'm going blind as well.'

'You can hear,' Frankie yelled, 'and hear this. If I didn't love you I'd have been out of this house long ago. And if you don't like things here you can go back to the club where you said you were bored to tears. Or get yourself a housekeeper like Sullivan who, he told me, cheats him right, left and centre.'

'It's all a distant roaring, her voice,' Barney groaned. 'In all the years she's never learned pitch and modulation. It must be because she comes from Kerry. I can understand her anger. She's frustrated, physical frustration. You'd think a doctor, a person who sets herself up as an expert on sex, would realize that, wouldn't you? Of course I forgive her. I understand. I don't want to be a burden to anyone. I'm just an old man defeated by disability and having to rely on the kindness of those who have reason to be kind to me. . . .'

'Oh yes. For all the diamonds and minks you gave me,' Frankie said. 'And the amount you've left me in your will.'

That must have struck home because Barney drew himself up regally and bowed to me.

'It's a good thing I didn't hear what she said. It was probably some cruel insult. As I don't wish to be a burden to you both I'll withdraw to my lonely room. I'm used to it. Loneliness.'

Followed by the lumbering Willy, Barney stalked off. Half way up the stairs he must have slipped because there was a loud curse and then the thud of him throwing off his slippers before falling into bed.

'Let's have another drink,' said Frankie. She looked, as usual, quite unscarred by Barney's tirade, merely remarking that he was always foul after a session with Sullivan. 'Both of them, Sullivan and Barney, retain their capacity for drink but forget that their poor old bladders aren't what they were,' she said, and reclined on a chaise longue sipping at her wine.

'Life's so ironic,' she went on. 'Here are you with a son and no husband and me with no children at all only a crusty old bastard who has the temperament of a prima donna and the hypochondriasis of a neurotic patient! The times I used to long for mad passionate love, to be whirled off by dashing lovers who'd fight a duel for me, or swept into a suitable marriage by a man who'd protect and look after me. I ask myself, why the hell do I stick with old Barney?'

I often asked myself that, too, but two glasses of wine emboldened me to say that Barney's mercurial temperament meant that whatever his irritations he never bored her. And, I added, if they didn't really care for each other, they wouldn't bother to fight. Their two personalities generated electricity but at least there was warmth and life, not like so many married couples who had a relationship like Brown Windsor soup.

'Maybe you're right,' Frankie yawned. 'God, I'm tired. Another stack of letters to do in the morning before I go to work.'

When I got home the hospital rang me. It was Lia, very apologetic because she said she knew that I wasn't on duty but she thought I'd want to know that Sheena Boden had been admitted to Parker ward a few hours ago in a very bad state.

'I saw her because I am on duty,' Lia said. 'But she is so psychotic that she didn't recognize me. She won't let anyone near

77

her and she is asking for you.'

'I'll be over,' I said. Fortunately the night although dark and with the chill of late October was clear and windless, and I got to Parker ward very quickly.

I could hear the high shrieking sound of Sheena before I got to the side room where she had been put. She stood in one corner, plucking at her torn white gown and the air was reeking with the smell of diabetic urine. Her face was pinched and chalk white and the pupils of her eyes were so dilated that they looked like pools of pitch. She shook uncontrollably and pointed at one corner of the room.

'It's there . . . the black thing . . . stop it coming closer. Oh God, my God . . .'

Whatever horror her poor crazed brain saw in the corner it was filling her with such fear that every time one of the four night nurses tried to come near her she pushed them away and continued to scream hoarsely. Then her staring eyes struggled to focus at me and she gave a shaky smile. But she still pointed at the corner of the room.

'Get one hundred milligrams of chlorpromazine,' I said to one of the nurses, 'and we'll give it to her right away.'

Sheena looked as if she hadn't slept for weeks. I couldn't believe the change in her. When she clutched me her hands felt cold and sweaty and her breath stank of the acetone caused by her diabetes.

'I want you to have an injection, Sheena,' I said. 'You need rest . . . a good sleep . . .'

'I can't while that thing . . . that in the corner . . .' She pointed again to whatever gruesome thing lurked there.

'The injection will take it away.' I took the syringe from the nurse.

'Now Sheena . . . Please . . . this will help you,' I said, and she allowed me to slide the needle into her without protest.

As the drug took effect she allowed herself to be put to bed and then pulled me down so that I could hear the whisper coming from her dry cracked lips.

'It's come again, the schizophrenia, hasn't it? I tried to keep well. Now they'll take Melinda away . . . all I've got . . .'

78

She was so exhausted that the drug took almost immediate effect and she slept.

13

The next day I had so many domiciliary visits to do that I didn't get time to visit Sheena till late afternoon. She'd slept all night and most of the morning, Logan told me, but was now bathed and able to drink the fluids she so badly needed. She still wouldn't take medication by mouth and was having to have massive doses of sedative drugs by intramuscular injection.

'Gone right back, hasn't she, poor kid?' said Logan sympathetically. 'Oh, Mrs Gibbons her social worker wanted to have a word with you. Here's her number.'

I said I'd see Sheena first and went along to her room. Even in twenty-four hours there was a change for the better in the girl's condition. A tiny nurse was gently encouraging her to sip milk from a beaker and Lia showed me her chart which indicated that her fluid balance was better and that her diabetes was coming under control.

'How are you, Sheena?' I sat down on the edge of the bed. Her eyes were still staring and every now and then she glanced around her suspiciously and her sore lips moved silently. She snatched my hand and her bones felt brittle and bird-like.

'It's as if I'm in a dark tunnel and I can't get out. And I seem to hear people talking to me, even when there isn't anybody there. I felt it coming on. I've gone mad again, haven't I, doctor? And I did everything I was told. I had my injections and I rested as much as I could. I'd wanted to come and see you but I was afraid they'd take Melinda away. And now they have and maybe I'll never see her again . . .'

Tears slid down her cheeks. How flaccid her skin was, hanging in dry folds like an old woman's. She looked twenty years older.

'Mrs Gibbons is seeing to Melinda,' I said. 'I'm going to talk to her in a few moments and I'll let you know the news right away.

But I want you to do something for me. I want you to take your medicine because it's going to make you better and we don't want to have to keep injecting you.'

The idea of a needle however sharp having to pierce the matchstick limbs was terrible.

'I want to get better. I don't want to lose Melinda. So I'll take my tablets.'

'And I want you to have some ECT as well.'

'Must I?'

'If you want to get better, Sheena.'

'All right. I wish . . .' She lunged forward and stared fixedly at the corner of the room which had so frightened her last night. 'I wish that black thing would go away. It gets bigger and bigger. Even when I shut my eyes I can see it.'

'That's because you're ill,' I said. 'Have a sleep now and take your tablets when the nurses bring them to you.'

I told Lia to set up ECT for Sheena as soon as possible and I went back to the office and phoned Mrs Gibbons. I liked Mrs Gibbons. She was a small middle-aged woman who had been a nurse herself and was a rare mixture of common sense, compassion and good humour.

Melinda had been placed with a couple known to the department for their skill in caring for children who'd been unsettled. Her mother's illnesses didn't seem to have upset Melinda so far, but as Mrs Gibbons said, you had to wait and see.

'Meantime, she's being very well cared for. How long do you think the mother's going to be ill, Doctor?'

I said it was impossible to be very definite. The girl was suffering from two grave illnesses. In that case, said Mrs Gibbons, the department had best assume parental rights.

'That doesn't mean adoption?' I asked.

'Oh, no. Simply what it says, that we, the Social Services, have parental rights over the child purely till the mother is able to look after her.'

'Because Sheena is determined to have her child back,' I said. 'And it would impede her recovery to think that there was any doubt about that.'

'No question of adoption at this stage,' said Mrs Gibbons. 'But

81

of course we have to protect the welfare of the child, don't we, Doctor?'

'And of the mother,' I said. 'The two are connected.'

'Well, we must have a meeting about this when Sheena is a bit better. It's terribly sad, I mean the fact of the girl being so alone and not having any family at all.'

'Except Melinda,' I said.

Nice as Mrs Gibbons was I could see that she was embroiled in bureaucracy and I knew that when Sheena got better, as I was sure she would, then she would have to fight hard to get her child back. When I returned to tell her that Melinda was happily placed she was asleep. The nurse reported that she had taken her tablets orally and I knew there'd be no more need for injections.

A calendar on the wall caught my eye. My God, tonight was when I was down for addressing the parents at St Bede's and I hadn't done a scrap of preparation. I hadn't made a note, looked up books or asked anyone's advice. Frankie was useless because things like public speaking and promoting herself were so easy for her. I often thought she'd have been good in advertising or PR work, and she could easily have made a living out of her culinary and artistic talents. I knew where I'd get help though. Tony Manners had three children and he was so avant garde in his psychiatry that he'd know how and what to put across. Besides, he'd worked for two years in a child guidance clinic.

'It's not the children you have to instruct, it's the parents,' he said when I'd tracked him down finishing his lunch in the canteen. 'Christ, there must be a Borgia in the kitchen, the curry's vile.' He pushed his plate away and began to peel an orange.

'But I thought people knew everything about sex now,' I said.

'You'd be surprised at the number of unconsummated marriages there still are,' Tony said. 'And the first night fumbling and bumbling! What you've got to realize is that these Mums and Dads – and I bet most of the Dads stay away from your meeting – only know the crude mechanics which they dodge telling the kids about because anyway they don't know the right words. They're more embarrassed than the kids, see?'

'Then there's Father Mortimer. He's rather staid and doesn't want me to use words that are too crude.'

'Oh, God,' said Tony, 'of course it's a Catholic school, isn't it? That makes a difference. For God's sake keep clear of the Virgin Birth because that'll really flummox the kids. Now look, what you'll do, you've brought up a son of your own, haven't you? That'll give you a guide.'

I wasn't too sure about that, I said, because when I'd explained the process of birth to my son he'd asked whether, if the mothers didn't like their new babies, they could stuff them back in again, and when I'd said no, certainly not, he'd seemed to lose interest.

'Well, I'm sure you'll be all right,' said Manners. 'All the Irish have the gift of the gab.'

'But not about sex. That's our national hang up,' I said. 'And partly responsible for our high alcoholic rate.'

Still, there was nothing I could do about things now. No question of opting out. No matter what sort of mess I made of things I couldn't let Father Mortimer down. I'd just have to see what the others said, especially the lady teacher, Mrs Marriot, and try and vamp my way through.

On my way down to see 'Hatchet Man' Ingham I met Frankie charging towards me, her tote bag crammed with letters and papers, making her look like a postwoman.

'How's Barney?' I asked.

'Flourishing. Why wouldn't he be with the care he takes of himself. It's me that feels panned out.' She really did look whacked. There were shadows under her eyes and even the bold application of blusher couldn't hide her pallor.

'Twenty more bloody letters this morning,' she said. 'I'm working till two in the morning and I can't keep up. The unanswered piles of mail haunt me and I'm running out of replies. I'm starting to lean on 'I'd advise you to see your doctor' which is rich, as they've written to one. Of course Sir senses this, and he's beginning to gloat and say he knew I wouldn't be equal to it. And he keeps bringing up nasty things like what would happen if I died and these letters were found among my effects? Or what if one of the sex nuts discovered where I lived?'

'Take no notice,' I said, 'and bash on. There's always the money.'

'That's just it,' said Frankie, looking worried. 'I haven't had any money yet. I wrote to the editor twice and just had one vague letter and nothing else.'

'They're probably a bit casual,' I said, 'like their sex.'

'Come for a meal on Saturday and tell me all about your thing tonight,' she said.

No, I said, it was high time I gave dinner to herself and Barney so she said that Saturday night next would be fine.

'Though as usual I can't guarantee what Sir's mood will be like,' Frankie called after me.

It didn't matter. The great thing about Barney's up-and-down temperament was that the dark clouds invariably lightened, and I knew from experience that if Frankie was down as she was now, Barney would be up.

When I saw Ingham he seemed much calmer and more composed and told me that he no longer heard voices. When I asked him about the hatchet and Charlie Hazel he smiled enigmatically although I was slightly consoled to read in the notes of a former hospital where he'd been a patient six years ago that he'd been threatening at that time to 'do' Hazel with a hatchet. Detective-Sergeant Mills agreed with this when I rang him and said that in spite of his violent talk there had never been trouble from Ingham and he'd had plenty of opportunities as he knew where Hazel lived.

*   *   *

I thought I'd try and get home early to write some headings for tonight's talk at the school but all my plans for relaxation were dissipated when I arrived back and found a white card lying on the door mat. In wobbling but clear black capitals were printed the words I'M GOING TO GET YOU DELANEY

I tried to concentrate on what I was going to say to the parents but I kept wondering who could have sent that card. Was it Ingham? Had he found out I'd gone to the police? Or was there some psychopathic patient who had a paranoid grudge against me lurking in the community somewhere?

I wasn't too much a coward but I made sure to check that all doors and windows were shut properly before setting off for St Bede's school. It was tucked up a narrow winding lane incongruously called 'Lovely Lane' in an area of Rigton which abounded in factories, tanneries and gas-works. I recognized Father Mortimer's old car and made out two nuns scurrying towards the front door. It was hard to know their ages because they had the perennial innocent-looking youthfulness that nuns always do have.

Father Mortimer was standing in the hall surrounded by a group of crimplene clad parish ladies whilst a few children stood giggling at the entrance of the small school hall just behind us.

There was the remembered school smell of ink and polish and bodies and then Father, like Dracula in his long cape and soutane, grasped my hands.

'So very good of you to come, Doctor. Mrs Marriot, our senior teacher . . .' A plump trim little woman tripped forward and shook hands with me.

'Mr Vickers, the headmaster.' He was small and balding with the anxious sedate air of a family solicitor or a bank manager. To my horror I saw that all three of them, Father included, were holding a sheaf of notes.

14

The two nuns were introduced as Sister Imelda and Sister Monica. Sister Imelda was freckled and young and Sister Monica was a doctor working in South America and both of them laughed in that way nuns have which can only be described as 'merry'. A trickle of parents looking a bit awkward as if they were late for Mass made their way past us into the hall, most of them nodding to or greeting Father and the two teachers.

'Quite a gratifying attendance,' Father Mortimer said beside me. 'Quite encouraging. Ah . . . good evening, Father.'

A tubby little man with a mop of wild red hair shook Father Mortimer's hand with friendly joviality. This was Father Moran, the priest of Rigton's other parish. He was an 'ordinary' as opposed to being a member of the rather exclusive monastic order that Father Mortimer and his colleagues belonged to, and, like Father Mortimer, he was the despair of his cardiologist because he worked so hard. Again like Mortimer he was a traditionalist and disliked the dropping of the Mass in Latin and the easy-going, not to say unorthodox, ways of the new young curates. I saw him give Father Michael Mason, who had just come in, a disapproving look. I understood why. Mason, dressed in a white turtle-necked sweater, pale grey suede jacket and dark grey slacks, could have been a model for a male boutique.

Vickers rushed up and tapped his watch. 'Well, time's getting on. We've got about thirty-four parents, Father. Should we start?'

'To be sure, to be sure,' Father said. Before striding forward he murmured to me, 'I do hope you'll find what I've done is of assistance to you, Doctor. I've had the diagrams and charts from the Marriage Guidance clinic put up on the wall behind the dais as it will save you having to use the blackboard for any diagrams you may wish to make.'

About six rows of people were arranging themselves on plastic chairs as Father, Mr Vickers and Mrs Marriot and myself went towards the dais on which there were four chairs and a table. As predicted there were more women and girls than men. The nuns sat in the front row and Father Mason, looking bored, placed himself at the back on a chair near the door.

All of a sudden I was conscious of the huge and wildly coloured drawings depicting the human reproductive process which were attached like some mad mural to the wall behind us. There was a penis of tremendous proportions framed by two testicles like footballs. The next diagram showed semen or as Father would have it 'the seed of love' shooting out of an erect phallus like pellets from a Sten gun. Yet another diagram depicted a mountainous uterus with ovarian tubes floating out on each side in a most peculiar way. Then there was the gravid uterus in various stages of growth, the coiled foetus looking like a malevolent little old man. There was something odd about that uterus. I found myself staring at it and trying to recall my rusty gynaecology. It wasn't that rusty. This uterus or womb was placed upside down. I pulled at Father's sleeve just as Mr Vickers had got to his feet to welcome us all and thank the speakers for giving of their time.

'Father Mortimer!' Thank God he was beside me and I didn't have to lean across Vickers. 'Father,' I whispered more urgently.

'What is it? What is it? Dear me, I've just discovered that I've brought the notes of my sermon for Sunday instead of my notes for this evening. Yes, what is it?'

'That diagram . . . of the . . . er . . . womb. . . . It's upside down.'

'What?'

I nodded as discreetly as I could towards the misplaced organ. 'It's upside down, the womb.'

Father Mortimer sighed and clicked his tongue. The children had put up the diagrams, he said and didn't it just show their innocence, poor dears? 'We'll just have to hope that there are no doctors in the audience and even if there are then I'm sure they'll understand,' he whispered. 'What does it matter anyway as long as the general idea is right?'

87

I'd have loved to say that it would certainly have mattered to the Blessed Virgin, but Mr Vickers was just finishing off his preamble and turning to introduce Father Mortimer.

The priest stood up, stooped and frail looking, and after searching for his spectacles in both pockets and then finding them on the table in front of him he said that he was afraid he'd forgotten his notes.

'I might think it was incipient dementia,' he said, 'except for the fact that I've always been absent-minded and took a sleeping tablet instead of a heart tablet during Holy Mass last week, most embarrassing as the Bishop was giving the sermon. However, there are things we must not be vague about and that's why we're here tonight. Our children are being subjected to a persistent and pernicious stream of sex from a variety of sources. And much of it isn't normal sex but violence and depravity clothed in lust. The Catholic Church has been remiss in not instructing and preparing our children to be strong enough to resist this indoctrination. We should not seek to cram children with precocious information before they are ready but equally we shouldn't fail them when they *are* ready and that, my dear people, that is not the school's job. They can help but it is for the parents to inform their children of the facts of life and not funk it and abrogate their responsibilities to the teachers or, worse still, have our little ones pick things up by beastly whispers and play-time jokes. There's always some youngster who thinks he knows more than others and although it may not be, and very often isn't, the correct version, this child is only too anxious to impart his wisdom and so children are incorrectly informed and tell their parents that they know about everything. We don't want our children to lose their innocence but neither do we want them to be dangerously ignorant.'

Father's voice rose and fell passionately. The two nuns looked at their toes. Some parents looked guilty and you knew they had what Father called 'funked things', whilst others looked rather smugly self-satisfied, having, I supposed, done their stuff about the birds and bees.

Mrs Marriot stood up after the applause following Father Mortimer had died down. How clearly written her notes were, how right the line she took. She would confine herself to what she knew, she said, and that was the remarks and questions of the eleven-year-old children that she taught. Some knew a great deal about biology and others less, but all of them were curious. They wanted to know about the birth process, how the baby was nourished, miscarriage, the Pill and even, she added greatly daring, even abortion. The children who had had sex instruction from their parents were obviously better adjusted as well as better informed and she would agree with Father that it was the parents', not the teachers', job to tell their children about sex.

Mrs Marriot then gave several light and amusing examples of what her class of children had said about the facts of life. There was nothing sordid or shocking in any of her discourse. The horrific diagrams were never referred to and she concentrated on the bits about the joys of motherhood and young fathers helping with the babies and the virtues of breast feeding. She never attempted to mention the difficult bits about how the seed actually got into the mother and why people had intercourse at all. I couldn't help thinking that it would be beyond any child to imagine how people could get pleasure from the insertion of that massive penis in the diagram into the upside-down womb!

'I have left the . . . er . . . more technical aspects in the capable hands of Doctor Delaney.' Mrs Marriot smiled sweetly and sat down with a rustle of her taffeta petticoat.

I stood up very conscious of the violently coloured diagrams in the background and I said that I was of a generation and a race which had suffered cruelly and unnecessarily from a lack of sex instruction. There had been plenty of nods, winks and innuendoes and nothing more. Beyond a necessary but still insufficient warning about menstruation, we were told nothing. It was only the strict religious code with which we were indoctrinated that kept us from being permanently pregnant or infected with VD. So I was a casualty from lack of sex instruction and I wouldn't want other young people to suffer as I had done.

I surprised myself by the fluency with which I spoke. I couldn't force myself to use Father Mortimer's euphemisms of 'tassels' for penises – and I ignored the crude diagram. I spoke about the importance of stressing love and self-respect when talking about sex. I gave my views of abortion, masturbation, premarital sex, birth control and only the rather stern look on Father Mortimer's face decided me to shut up. Maybe I was boring people by indulging my own views too much but I saw the two nuns smiling, so that encouraged me.

'Like to thank the doctor for a most stimulating talk. Perhaps we may continue the dialogue over some tea.'

Four small girls carrying large trays of plastic beakers of tea appeared and people began to cough and whisper amongst themselves.

'Who would like to kick off?' Vickers hopped to his feet like an eager gnome.

Father Moran at the back, who had been writing during the talks, cleared his throat, got to his feet and stuck his fingers in his black waistcoat.

'Our speakers have all given us much to think about. Much to think about,' he said. 'But aren't we all making too much out of this sex thing? A few words from the parents, yes, but the average child will pick things up as he goes along and at his own pace. I don't hold with this modern idea of cramming kids full of sex. 'Tis only giving 'em ideas. Much better keep 'em occupied by playing games. Especially boys. 'Tis like this modern craze for eating meat twice and three times a day. Long ago we used only to have it once a week and I can tell you it was a real treat. What I'm saying to ye is this. Dere's too much made out of sex these days. It did us no harm at all to keep our innocence for as long as we could in Ireland. There used to be a ting called "modesty" in the girls. 'Twas only the very odd girl in the parish that would be seen pregnant without a husband.'

'That's because you packed them all over to England to have their babies over here and damn the help they got from their village in Ireland, so, often, the poor things had to go on the streets and become prostitutes to earn enough money to eat.' The speaker was a lean man with frizzy hair, spectacles and a beard. 'I agree that children should have sexual instruction,' he went on, 'and why the hell shouldn't they learn that sex is enjoyable and good and the most wonderful thing two people can do? I come from a small Welsh village where nobody gave you actual instruction like but you picked things up from some generous girl. It was called Sitting Next To Nelly.'

Mr Vickers looked outraged, Father Mortimer jumped to his feet and Father Moran shouted, 'Dat's de sort of talk I object to. It's that sort of filty remark which would bring a blush to the cheek of God and His Holy Mother. And you call yourself a Catholic, sir?'

'No, I don't,' said the bearded man, 'and the reason I don't is because the Church has too many people like you in it.'

Poor Father Mortimer waved his arms desperately and Father Moran, after giving a ferocious glare at the bearded one, sat glowering down at his shoes.

'I was brought up in the country,' said a pleasant-faced girl in a red cape and black stockings, 'and we learned about sex from animals. It was all quite beautiful and natural.'

'Well, I don't know,' said a fat blonde who was dragging fiercely at a cigarette. 'Maybe it's different in the country but my lads keep watching the rabbits and asking why they're Always At It? And as regards it being natural, well I seen dogs do disgusting things, with their own sex.'

'I think we're getting bogged down by details,' Father Mortimer said. 'Let us try not to be personal or aggressive and keep to the main themes. I mean we all agree that children need to know about sex, don't we? It follows from that that they must be taught that sex is too wonderful and sacred and . . .'

'No, we're not,' said a dumpy woman who had taken out her knitting and was working away beside the two nuns.

'Not what, Mrs Fletcher?'

'I'm not agreed that I should have to tell kids about sex. I think God must have been off his rocker when he invented it. I did my duty by my husband but don't tell me it were more than that. I had ten kids; they're all married and doing well and I never told any of 'em a damn thing.'

Mrs Fletcher 'did' for Father Moran and I could see from the way he smiled at her that what she'd said pleased him.

'But Mrs Fletcher,' said poor Father Mortimer, 'didn't you get a most awful shock when you were first married? Would you subject others to that?'

'Yes, I did,' said Mrs Fletcher, clashing her needles. 'What with the heat of Arthur, and the weight of him, and the smell of stale porter, I thought the dawn would never come.'

Any attempts of Father Mortimer to bring the discussion to a more elevated plane were lost after Mrs Fletcher's heart-felt outburst. There was a rather fraught moment when Mason got up after the laughter following Mrs Fletcher had died down, and Father Mortimer tapped his foot nervously as his young curate, bizarrely incongruous with his Rupert Brooke profile and elegant clothes, said that didn't we think that we were all overdoing our fears about sexual ignorance and shouldn't we keep our sense of humour about things?

'I remember a boy at school swearing to tell us absolutely everything about sex when the teacher had gone out,' he said. 'He went up to the blackboard, we all trembled in anticipation and all he drew was a pair of ladies' legs.'

Mr Vickers, glancing at his watch, said we'd run out of time but not of enthusiasm and he'd like to thank us all so much for coming and we would all go home with a lot to think about.

I shot out quickly. I felt I'd rather let down Father Mortimer by being too earthy and I was glad his attention was taken up chatting to Father Moran. The two nuns joined me in walking to the cars and said that they'd enjoyed my talk very much.

'Poor Father Mortimer,' said Sister Imelda, laughing, 'his intentions are of the best but he hasn't got very far from the gooseberry bush era.'

'I'm afraid I was distracted by that uterus on the diagram,' remarked the other. So Monica's keen eyes had taken that in! 'And the ovum was going up the wrong way too.'

15

Sheena spent the next few days sleeping, and gradually she grew calmer, less apprehensive and frightened, and she stopped complaining of the petrifying black spot in the corner of the room. The ECT and the drugs had dragged her back from her horrendous hell.

I hadn't time to ponder on the St Bede's night because my clinics were very busy. I didn't finish my Friday one till nearly seven o'clock and was standing outside one of the many entrances to the hospital battling with a resistive umbrella when a taxi drew up and a furious-looking little woman ejected a shabby little bundle of a man who blinked in the slashing rain.

'Here,' said the woman, shoving the small man at me, 'you take him, I don't want him.' Then she leaped back in the taxi and shot off.

I was left again with poor old Billy Keane whose only crime was that he'd grown old and useless and spent his time sitting like a cabbage all day, too beaten by life to wash and feed himself. Mrs Keane, after forcing him to sign over his pension to her, had no further time for him and she made it clear that she didn't want him home 'cluttering up the place' as she said, and being entirely unproductive. Every time I tried to discharge him from the long-stay ward at Barrington Hall, which was the only home he'd known in recent years, she managed to get him back into hospital by making him so miserable at home, with her jeers and taunts plus her ultimate weapon of not feeding him, that he'd made pathetic attempts at suicide by swallowing aspirins, and had himself admitted to hospital again. She'd never gone so far as actually dumping him like this though. There was nothing for it but to put him in my car and drive him to his old ward. Getting an ambulance would take too long, and anyway I was going back to Barrington Hall. Mr Keane followed me with the cowed look of a beaten dog, and in the car I noticed the huge bump on his shaggy white head. How had it happened, I asked him?

'The wife hammered me last night,' he said, with the fatalistic air of someone to whom violence is run of the mill. 'I spilled some milk, see, and then the TV went queer, so she flew into a rage and she told me she'd put me back in the nut-house and that I wasn't ever to come home again and mess things up.'

'It's your house as well, Billy,' I said, wondering if there were any homes for battered husbands.

'She don't look at it like that,' he said with resignation.

Mr Hood, the male nurse, was not at all pleased to see poor Mr Keane, as his old place on a back ward had been filled, and Billy would have to sleep in the acute admission ward for the moment.

'It's that wife of his ought to be in, Doc,' Hood said. 'Billy's all right. Isn't it awful that a man has to end up in a psychiatric hospital because there's just nowhere for him to go?'

I agreed. Poor Billy Keane represented one of the new group of people who posed far more trouble than the really mad who could be helped by the new drugs. Women were working, homes were small, society was moving faster and faster. Hospitals for the subnormals were crammed, as were the prisons, and the Sally Army seemed to have beaten a retreat.

'And the police won't keep tramps or drunks in the cells any more,' Hood added.

So all the people who weren't really insane or evil, but too dull or slow to fit into the community, were nobody's responsibility and ended up, like Keane, with us, and we had no facilities, with open doors and a therapeutic atmosphere, to lock these people up, nor did we have the legal right to stop them if they wanted to go.

'Oh, Billy won't want to go,' Hood said. 'He's not daft. Who'd want to go back to a wife like his?'

Talking of inadequates reminded me to tell Hood that Ignatius O'Halloran was not to be re-admitted. He had a problem, but he wasn't mentally ill, and we weren't a charitable institution. What Mr O'H wanted was somewhere like that monastery in Ireland where the monks spent their time doing a most effective drying-out process on drunks. That's what nuns and monks were really good at, I thought, looking after the sick, the old and the unwanted, and God knows we needed it in an age where people shouted 'Something must be done' at the doctors. 'I need help' was the cry of the seventies, which had taken the place of the 'I'm looking for an identity' of the sixties.

But what about people like Violet Baker? I went from Mr Hood's ward up to one of the back wards to see whether big Violet was there or not. She was a large, simple-minded woman, whose only sister wanted nothing to do with her. Violet wasn't mad, nor was she very subnormal. She was an eccentric. Social Services had tried to help her, but she took no notice, striding through the streets, affronting people by her vacant look, her tatty old clothes and her smell.

'Dunno what Vi does when she goes out to get that smell,' said Sister Benson, the beaming West Indian Sister of the ward where Violet was generally accommodated when she came in to us. 'She looks clean enough, but she gets this awful smell. Then she goes sleeping rough at the railway station and the police send her up here.'

'And we keep her till she hikes off again,' I said.

'She's no trouble. Really a lovely person is Vi,' Sister said. She explained that in Jamaica, someone like Vi would just have been allowed to walk around after being fed. So they would in this country thirty years ago, I said. But what happened to tramps and tinkers and gypsies these days?

'She disappeared two nights ago. What'll I do if she turns up again, Doctor?' Sister asked. 'She'll only last so long and then she'll arrive here stinking and hungry and with blisters on her heels.'

'Then let her have a bed and give her something to eat,' I said.

The nurses must have me down as a softie, a real softie, I thought, and when I reached Sheena's ward I knew it. I was to take deep breaths, Sister Logan told me, Emma Flaxton had been brought in during the night.

'She's swallowed a bottle of tablets bought at Boots, and arrived up here escorted by two Pandas, from St Peter's. She won't go to the ward that Sister Benson was on, and we've only two beds left here.'

'Bring me a cup of coffee and then Emma,' I said. 'But bring the coffee first.'

A bustling young nurse brought in some coffee and I tried to think what to do about Emma. She wasn't quite so bright and she was certainly far more annoying and trying than Violet, who just wanted silently to stride around, stinking, but otherwise bothering no one. It wasn't her fault really, if her wild untidiness and smell offended her fellow humans. But Emma was a different matter. To begin with, she was older, and she wasn't as strong as Vi. She also chattered non-stop and had a knack, that she'd brought almost to an art, of offending people. In between her stays at Barrington Hall, where she really didn't fit in as she wasn't suffering from a psychiatric condition, merely lack of intelligence and an inability to cope with life in the outside world, she had been offered so many flats and places in homes, which she'd turned down, that the Social Services, after straining their resources to the utmost, had written to me to say they were washing their hands of Emma. GPs too, fed up with her haunting their surgeries and calling them out at terrible hours, had all refused to have her as a patient, and now she was being 'shared' by a pool of GPs, each putting up with her for a stint of three months at a time.

'But she's got a low cunning, Emma,' Sister Logan said. 'She had a hundred pounds on her when she came in. And you know she has a flat provided by the Council, but she says she doesn't like it because the neighbours avoid her. So she swallowed the tablets to get in here.'

I could perfectly appreciate why her neighbours avoided Emma. She waddled in, clutching an inadequate hospital dressing-gown around her barrel-shaped body, chubby face made plumper by her Dutch Doll hair cut, and she never stopped talking. I just sat and let the torrent of words pour over me.

'I felt that low, Doctor, I didn't know what to do with myself. Where's me cloak, Sister?'

She didn't wait for Logan to tell her but went on.

'I went down to the Social and they didn't do nothing, and then I got on a bus and it was going the wrong way, and the girl

96

at the check out in the supermarket called me an old cow, so I went to the police about her and there was this red-faced policeman and he was terrible. So I went to St Peter's after taking the tablets. I tried to get me own doctor first, but them receptionists is awful. Can I stay in this ward, Doctor? I like it here.'

I made my voice as Coulterish as I could, and said that no, she couldn't stay on this ward. There was nothing mentally wrong with her, no disease, and we weren't a hostel, and she had a flat outside.

She burst into loud bawls, and I could feel my blood pressure shooting up as I had to shout, too.

'Shut up, Emma, that doesn't impress me,' I said.

The tears stopped as they so easily did with Emma, because she had no deep feelings, everything was superficial.

'You can still have a bed on Sister Benson's ward,' I said. 'And that's being generous.'

'Wa, wa,' Emma wailed. 'I'm not going there. I hate that Sister. She tells me off and she makes me eat things I don't like. And she shouts something awful at me. I hate her.'

'That's too bad then, Emma,' I said.

'I'm going home,' screeched Emma, 'and I might take more tablets. Where's me cloak?'

'If you come back you'll go to Sister Benson's ward,' I warned her.

So Emma, after wrapping her cloak around her, waddled off, looking like some fat witch without a broomstick. I did feel a pang of remorse when she tried to press a wad of notes in my hand, saying she was willing to pay if she could stay in Parker ward.

'I'm practising being a toughie,' I said to Coulter over lunch the next day. His first name was Ivan but nobody ever called him that for some reason. Perhaps it was his air of antiseptic remoteness.

'I don't have to try,' he said. 'The NHS has just so much resources which are being depleted by the exploiting brigade that you've been telling me about. We're not a doss-house, or a hostel or a lodging place. D'you know it costs more to keep a patient here than it does a boy at Eton?'

'Only they have a better time here,' said Manners sitting down at our table.

'I met a weird little woman who says she's a patient of yours, Joyce. Says she's off to Boots to get more tablets.'

'And I expect she'll arrive back tonight having been washed out at St Peter's and with two Panda cars escorting her,' I said.

'No real reason for keeping her if she just wants digs,' Tony Manners went on. 'It is quite wrong. It isn't being charitable, not really.'

'I'd get all the drunks, bums and layabouts to bloody work and stop all this skiving and scrimshanking,' Coulter added.

I left them to their usually equable dialogue, and went down to the clinic to discover my first patient was someone whom Coulter would probably have liquidated if he could!

Benjamin Olive was an intelligent, though unfortunate, product of an English girl falling for an American GI during the last war. He was a thin rasher of a man, with a handsomeness which, like everything else about Benjamin, failed dismally because his nose had been broken or fractured so many times by falls, and one of his blue-black eyes had a bad squint; and because he'd never bothered to get his teeth fixed after someone had, as he said, 'took a poke at him' in a pub, half his very good front teeth were missing. Benjamin's epileptic fits were genuine, but he was bright enough to simulate them at will, and many a young houseman and nurse had laboured over him thinking that they were dealing with a cardiac arrest or a status epilepticus when Benjamin was really hamming it up. If he'd had better health and more will-power he'd have made quite a good second-rate actor. His sexuality was as misleading as his appearance, because he'd married a very dull plain girl, who'd produced four very good-looking and intelligent children by him. But Benjamin drank, smoked what I suspected was more than what he described as 'the odd joint', got picked up by gay men and had more than a nodding acquaintanceship with the police. His forte was attempted suicide and he'd been treated at various Casualties for trying to kill himself by poisoning, drinking caustic soda, slashing his wrists, and on one occasion he'd narrowly missed a vital artery with a shotgun. I had to keep reminding myself that his

98

mother had run off and left him at Euston Station. That he'd been jostled from foster home to foster home, that he'd been given a leucotomy, that his wife was nearly subnormal and that his whole life, partly through his inadequate messing up, was a shambles. The trouble was that Benjamin agreed. His real love had been ladies' hairdressing, he said, but who wanted someone who fell in a fit whilst dealing with a client? And when he'd been in hospital, as he had on many occasions, he'd done ladies' hair with enormous style and finesse. In spite of his ambivalent sexuality, or perhaps because of it, Benjamin was very popular with the women, and Sister whispered to me that he'd had a curvy girl in a yellow two piece, wiggling up and down outside.

I tried not to let my eyes linger too long on his awful clothes. He wore a wide sombrero slanted on his narrow brown face, his shabby sheepskin coat swept around his bright yellow boots, and there were numerous silver bangles on his narrow, scarred wrists.

'What is it now, Benjamin,' I asked wearily. I didn't have to look at the huge casenotes in front of me. I knew Benjamin's story off by heart. And I knew him enough to know that he was here because he was in trouble. At least he didn't try to con me with the patter about being a 'deprived child' and 'looking for a meaning' and 'everything going against me'.

'Well.' His hand flapped limply. 'Well, Doctor, I got a shaking up last week, from the police.'

'What for? Possession of cannabis? Or stealing?'

He giggled nervously and began a long rambling account of how he'd been walking in Electric Street. The name was as unlikely as his appearance, but there was such a street in the city, I knew. He'd been walking along when a 'friend' had come up to him, and before they knew where they were a policewoman had asked them to come to the station.

'And they charged you?'

'No, charged me friend. He had cannabis in a match box . . .'

Suddenly I noticed the over-bright shining eyes, the lop-sided smile and the weaving gestures, and I knew that he was as high as a kite on marijuana.

'Benjamin, have you been smoking pot before coming here?' I

asked.

'Just a joint. I was feeling that nervous, Doctor, and my wife has left me. And Social won't do anything more for me and I was thinking you might put in a word for me with Mr Godley, the Probation Officer.'

'What, for being in trouble over pot?'

'It wasn't me, it was this friend. I only spoke to him and this policewoman nabbed me before I knew where I was.'

Before he had a chance to throw one of his 'turns' I bundled him out to where his sultry girl friend was ogling a young male patient, moving gum rhythmically with her pale purple lips.

'Don't try and waste my time, Benjamin,' I said. 'Booze was bad enough, mixing it with your anticonvulsant tablets, but you come here full to the eyeballs with pot and expect me to give you the magic pill, the happy pill. Out. I have some calls to make.'

He was so surprised that he sloped off, looking over his shoulder like some bizarre and broken-down cowboy from a cheap 'B' Western picture.

I felt that I was advancing in learning Coulter tactics. The difference between me and him, though, was that he'd never have spoken to Benjamin after a few minutes sharp and perceptive questioning. Benjamin, like Vi and Emma, was a 'second' even amongst life's dirty linen.

16

I went to some trouble to make something special for Frankie and Barney on the Saturday night. I spent all afternoon preparing a chicken from a recipe I learned in Provence, I asked Coulter's advice on wine and I splurged on some extra special brandy. When my chicken was simmering satisfactorily and I'd arranged giant sprays of chrysanthemums in the sitting-room I felt quite pleased with myself. I didn't even need some of my Tio Pepe to elevate my spirits. Even my new hair-do pleased me. I'd been living like a hermit for too long I decided as I sprayed myself liberally with 'Joy'. My world was a limited one of dealing with mostly desperate people and I'd forgotten what even the vestiges of gracious living were like. Where were the dreams that Frankie and I had had as we gobbled cheap stodge in seedy cafés? I had yearned to hold a salon in a green and gold room in Paris, entertaining the intelligentsia, and Frankie had wanted the exultation of a mad and reckless love. Yet here we both were in our middle age, still pounding the medical beat and still hard up for money and without the support, emotional or otherwise, of understanding husbands.

But at least Frankie had Barney and tonight he showed his real kindness because Frankie was sunk in one of her rare moods of gloom. Her hair flopped limply around her washed-out face. She walked with a limp because her corns niggled her and even after two sherries there was none of the old flash and sparkle.

'Gone right down. Willy goes like this at times,' Barney told me when poor Frankie had hauled herself upstairs because she'd developed cystitis on top of her other troubles.

'This bloody caper with the magazine's killing her. The buggers haven't paid her yet, you know. And that bastard Cousins has taken to his bed with bronchitis. Oh, no, poor Frankie's not

101

the woman she was. I'm glad you asked us over tonight. She needs some diversion. Not herself at all.'

But Barney looked exuberantly healthy. His skin and hair shone, he was wearing his best Prince of Wales check suit and there was a red carnation in his button hole.

'Some wine, pet,' he greeted her return. 'It's a good one and it'll warm your blood. Come on, love.'

While Frankie arranged herself, legs up, in a reclining position on the settee Barney hovered around her urging her to sip the wine. After she had downed two glasses, and thinking of my chicken dish, I suggested we eat; she felt restored enough to pull a mirror out of her hand-bag and tell us that for the first time in weeks she felt hungry, even though, she concluded after another despairing peep into her mirror, she looked like the Wreck of the Hesperus.

At dinner Barney was in his glory. It was as if Frankie's deflation had rejuvenated him. I'd seen it before. Frankie, normally the dominant one, was yet subject to what she called her Celtic Twilights and then Barney came into his own, his batteries recharged by Frankie's vulnerability. It was this symbiotic see-saw that helped to keep the relationship going.

'I congratulate you on the meal, Joyce. And the wine. Yes, certainly, I'll dispense the port.'

Even Willy choosing to vomit under the table just at this moment couldn't dispel Barney's conviviality and Frankie, although still torpid and passive, had a small smile on her face.

It vanished when Barney brought Willy out to the kitchen to give him some water.

'I'm in terrible trouble, Joyce,' she said. 'I haven't told Barney. He knows that I haven't been paid for the *Urge* job but what he doesn't know is that I've lost the bloody brief case containing all the letters, and they're addressed to me. I think they were taken from my car, you know I never lock it. Christ, what'll I do if I'm blackmailed? Can you see the headlines in the paper?'

I could indeed. 'Pornographic letters found in lady doctor's car.' Newspapers always referred to women doctors as 'lady doctors'.

'I wonder where they are? Or who's taken them? Suppose the

poor bloody writers are blackmailed?'

Barney came back from the kitchen. 'No long faces,' he commanded. 'Come on, this port deserves attention. And the Stilton looks superb, Joyce.'

For someone who professed to get no taste from his food after some obscure affliction of his taste buds, Barney seemed to enjoy his dinner and he so set himself out to be amusing and charming that even Frankie began to smile and recover her ebullience.

'I tell her to forget about this bloody magazine lark and do some writing. Or broadcasting. She'd be marvellous on some of those chat programmes. The trouble with Frances is she's so many-talented it's hard for her to decide which one to use.'

Barney smiled and fondled Frankie's hand. 'Now forget all about those letters, Frankie,' Barney said, helping himself to some brandy. 'At the very worst we can exist on my salary and I've got some old shares that I can sell and we can take off for the Seychelles or somewhere.'

This was really something. I'd never heard Barney quite so carefree before.

'That would be lovely. Or Hawaii; I've always wanted to go there,' Frankie said. Suddenly she pointed to Willy who was heaving and gasping. He looked as if he was going to be sick again so we all went out to the kitchen where I managed to get down an old sack before the contents of Willy's stomach heaved up. Amongst the messy vomitus were bits of letters, handwritten on scraps of white, pink and green paper.

'It's my letters. The letters,' screamed Frankie. 'The bloody hound's eaten them.'

'Now, now,' said Barney soothingly. 'He found your open brief case on the floor and had a bit of a nibble at it.'

'Nibble, he's devoured everything! And you let me go through this worry and never opened your trap,' Frankie whirled on Barney.

'Listen,' he said. 'The work was too much for you. They're not going to pay you and Sullivan says it would be professional suicide for you to go to law, so just be thankful that Willy did you a favour.'

'Favour!' snorted Frankie. 'What if the firm come after me?'

'They won't. They can't. Forget about it.'

'Did you really mean what you said about the trip to the Seychelles?' Frankie was always quick to follow up an advantageous point.

'Why not? After all I don't have much more time, have I? I might as well do the little I can do before the wheel chair claims me completely.'

Frankie gave him a smacking kiss and said she'd hold him to that and I suggested another drink to take our minds away from the sight and smell of the paper-eating Willy.

It was as if Willy's regurgitation acted as a catharsis. Frankie, after Barney had charged her glass with brandy, recovered her spirits and decided to let the *Urge* venture fade into the gallery of some of her rather sordid memories. And Barney helped her by making more and more extravagant plans for their holiday. It didn't have to be the Seychelles or the South Seas, they could go to Samarkand or Tashkhent or Backchisherai. Flushed with wine and bonhomie, Barney gave us some James Elroy Flecker in a sonorous basso and Frankie, full of drunken admiration, whispered to me that of course Barney could have made his living as an actor, an opinion I'd heard her voice many a time in less happy moments when the Osborn acting ability was used to bewail his unhappy state of health.

'And now Frankie, you must give us "She walked through the fair". I'll only get the odd word of course but it'll bring back memories.'

So Frankie, looking like a boozy Speranza, tossed back her majestic mane of hair and began to sing the lovely plaintive young girl's lament. It should have been ridiculous and embarrassing, like a raddled Hibernian Melba creaking through one of her farewell performances, but somehow it wasn't. Frankie's voice was still pure and true and when the last sorrowful notes died away Barney wiped tears from his eyes and said that it was so exquisite that his heart was pierced with sadness for the lost joys of listening to music, one of his dearest pleasures. For an encore Frankie gave us 'I dreamt that I dwelt in marble halls' and then 'The last rose of summer'.

We flopped back wrapped in warm melancholy for youth and

joy and hope and then Frankie, fully restored to scintillation, laughed and asked me how the hell I'd got on with my Birds and Bees talk at St Bede's? Inflamed by wine and my friends' urgent encouragement I regaled them with an account of the upside-down ovum and Mrs Fletcher's put-down of sex.

'Say it again . . . say it again! "What with the weight of him and the heat of him and the smell of stale porter . . . oh my God!"' Barney mopped tears of laughter from his eyes in a convulsion of joy.

'And I can imagine poor Father M's face and old Moran's expression,' Frankie spluttered, 'and Mason, with his tinted hair, looking superior.'

Barney began to laugh again, shaking like an old wheeze box, and Frankie said she'd have to go upstairs. Her bladder wasn't equal to this.

'You're not just saying this about taking a super holiday?' I said to Barney when Frankie had gone out. In spite of her ready rallying I thought my friend looked tired and drawn. You didn't age gradually, not some people anyway, and looking at Frankie's wobbling chins and the effort it took her to heave her bulk to her feet I had a frightening glimpse of how she'd look as an old woman. She's never had a holiday for years because Barney insisted that life in a hotel or anywhere amongst strangers would be unmitigated agony for him so Frankie had never left him. I didn't want my wine to be responsible for bibulous promises which Barney wouldn't honour. But I should have known my man.

'I'm not drunk. Or at least not that drunk,' he said. 'I'll book the tickets tomorrow. I've noticed how done in Frankie looks and in spite of our little differences I love her. Maybe because of them. She's got the biggest heart of any woman I know and she's the best company of anyone in the world, man or woman. Old Sullivan has this bitch of a housekeeper, you know, and she's always demanding presents and gifts. He's got so he's completely dependent on her and Sullivan has told me that she keeps asking what he's left her in his will.' Barney closed a wily eye. 'He says that the old bag will have a surprise. But Frankie never asks for anything. The only thing I worry about is that she'll meet someone younger, someone who can give her all the things I can't, and I don't mean money. That's why I get poisoned with jealousy.'

'I know that, Barney,' I said. 'But I know how fond Frankie is of you.'

'But it isn't fair,' he said passionately. 'I'm too old for her, twenty-five years too old. She's still a vigorous woman with natural desires. And she's never had much out of life. That bastard of a husband left her penniless and she's saved nothing for her old age. She'll have what I have but it isn't much.'

He swirled his brandy in one of my Waterford balloon glasses. I'd never heard him talk like this. I tried to look suitably impassive when he began again.

'Of course I'm still married. Mildred, that's my wife, is a good woman. Can't fault her really. But I've nothing in common with her. Nothing.'

I was glad when the phone went because I was still terrified that Barney might regret what he'd been telling me when morning sobriety arrived. Frankie was making a regal progress down the stairs when I picked up the receiver. It was Father Mortimer and I knew by the edge in his voice that something had happened. He thanked me in a perfunctory way for coming to the session at St Bede's and then went on to say that something very serious had happened. I might as well know because it was hardly a thing that could be kept quiet.

'Father Mason,' he said, 'he went to supper with some friends after St Bede's. I presume he had rather a lot to drink because that's the most charitable explanation of what happened after that.'

My imagination ran riot. Had Mason driven around Rigton nude on his motor cycle? Or written graffiti on the Church walls?

'He was found in what is known as a "compromising position" with a youth in one of the worst areas in the town.' Mortimer's voice sounded very old and very tired. I had to strain to hear it.

'The police have taken it up and it will be a court matter of course. I wouldn't mind but the boy's mother is a poor widow and the boy himself was a member of the Youth Club run by Father Mason. The Abbot is coming over tomorrow.'

'What will happen to Father Mason?'

'I expect he'll be sent for a year or two's penance to one of our remoter monasteries,' Mortimer said.

'I can't stand pouffes,' Barney grunted, after I'd told them what Father had said. 'Can't stand them. One night I went for a pee in a Paris nightclub and this poncy type began to paw me so I laid him out flat and then found out that the poor bastard was blind and trying to find his way out. Felt ghastly, I can tell you. But I hate the buggers. When I was at public school you were afraid to bend down, you really were.'

'But fancy sending Father Mason to an all male monastery,' Frankie giggled tipsily. 'Rather like sending coals to Newcastle.'

I was thinking exactly the same but my heart bled for poor old Father Mortimer. His efforts to help the sexual education of the parish children hadn't exactly taken off and now there'd be the scandal of Mason's misdemeanour.

'Can't see what they get out of it,' Barney ruminated drunkenly.

'Or what they get *into* it,' Frankie said, getting up with rather alcoholic dignity. She yawned mightily and said it was time for home.

'It's quite a walk,' I said.

'A cab. We'll order a cab,' said Barney in a lordly way. 'Old Sullivan uses this cabbie who suffers from insomnia and I've got his number.'

By the time the insomniac cabby had arrived Frankie was fast asleep and Barney prodded her gently awake and escorted her out like a tiny cavalier.

17

The gaiety of the night spent with Frankie and Barney made me realize how institutionalized I was getting. The hospital was becoming my world, my work my reality, to the exclusion of my personal life.

'I know I look like a burst paper bag,' Frankie told me a few days after the party when we met for a quick lunch in a local restaurant, 'but you don't look so hot yourself!'

'When Duggan comes back, and he will be back in a few weeks, I'll take off somewhere,' I said. What I'd really like would be to hole up in the Ritz or the Savoy or somewhere and have my meals brought up whilst I watched rubbish on television and took the telephone off the hook.

'Well I've got Sir to send for brochures and he's still hell bent on this trip to Southern Climes,' Frankie said. She looked dashing in a pale yellow turban and a black suit. She'd written to the *Urge* people to say she was giving up the job. 'They won't give me a bean but as Barney says, it's not worth trying to chase them up. But there's something else in the pipe-line. I wrote off to the local radio station saying wasn't there a spot for an experienced woman doctor to answer female queries and they've accepted me. I'm to start next week. It'll all be the usual questions about flushes and the Pill and whether men have the meno too, but I think I'll be equal to that. And they pay twenty quid a programme.'

'Now that's your style, Frankie,' I said, 'far more than *Urge*.'

'Yes,' she almost purred, 'Barney thinks so too. He's a pet really, isn't he? Just that he's so God awful jealous which is rather flattering really at our ages. Hey, what about Father Mason, any news?'

The Abbot had come down, calm and unflappable, and Mason

was due to be whisked off to a rural monastery where he would presumably spend his time doing penitential work.

'Bet he spends his time getting off with the young novices,' Frankie said.

I then told her about Joan Harris, whom I was going to see that afternoon at the clinic, that was if she turned up.

'She won't,' declared Frankie. 'And if she does it's just so she thinks it's better to go through the motions of keeping in with you. You worry too much, that's your trouble. Christ, we're only human, only trying to do a job, not spread The Gospel.'

'Must go,' she said, standing up. 'I've got to meet Sir at the travel agency. He's a bit crabby today because bloody William got into trouble yesterday for running off with a workman's lunch in the park, although how that animal can run with his arthritis I don't know. See you.'

'You've dropped something Frankie.' I picked up a very tricky looking black satin nightie which had slipped from her bag.

'That's to wow Barney,' she said. 'If he can't hear he can certainly see.' Then she sailed out of the restaurant.

Before self-pity at my own loveless state engulfed me, I rushed off to my clinic and saw Joan Harris, smart in a purple trouser suit, sitting waiting for me.

'Well?' I asked. 'How are things? You're still alive anyway.'

The impassive face slid into a joyless smile. 'You might say I'm existing, not living,' she said.

Silence. I could hear Dr Ashraf next door, a boisterous little Indian psychiatrist, peppering some unfortunate patient with his usual barrage of irrelevant questions about hotels and holidays. 'And how much did they charge? For a room with a bath? My goodness, very dear. Was there TV in the room?'

There was a faint mumble from the unfortunate patient who probably wanted to talk about his nerves, and Ashraf bellowed, 'What are you saying about your marriage? There are only two alternatives. Separate or soldier on. There is no third alternative.'

Well, every therapist to their own methods, I thought, and then to my amazement Joan told me she'd got herself a job.

'So you've postponed suicide for a while?'

'I wouldn't say that. The job just helps me to kill time. That's all. Any chance of getting the kids back?'

'I don't know. Not for a long time,' I said. 'You're at liberty to destroy yourself, I suppose, but not them. Surely you can see that?'

She shrugged. She was always shrugging. Then she looked at me with those elongated eyes and said she'd heard Sheena Boden was very ill and back in hospital.

'Like I said before,' she began to get up, 'she's got nothing and yet she wants to live and I want out. What a life.'

'It's all we've got,' I said. 'But look at Sheena who in spite of having been dealt some rotten cards is still willing to take part in the game.'

'I hope she makes it.' It was the first time I'd heard Joan make an unselfish statement. And she pushed her appointment card at me for me to write on it.

She actually wanted to come again? I gave her another appointment, but I was truly astonished. Oh, the girl's motives were probably coldly realistic. She didn't want to come, didn't want to see me, still intended to keep her rendezvous with death, but it was something, it was a start. Maybe it was my egotistical imagination but I detected a tiny bond of communication developing between us.

'Remember what I said,' I told her as she walked to the door, moving with the silent grace of some cat who would always walk by itself. 'Have the consideration to announce your intention to overdose before doing it.'

It sounded callous and cruel but she actually laughed.

'That's what they call black humour, isn't it? I never met a doctor like you.'

'And I never met a patient like you,' I said.

'I hate doctors.' There was actual passion in her voice. 'Stalking around like stuffed mummies. Never listen to you and try to shut you up with tablets. And the words they use. It's as if they think the patients are morons.'

This was good. This was real live emotion, even though uncomplimentary.

'Well, I try and listen. And I don't give you tablets.'

'No, but you give me hell sometimes.'

'Maybe that's what you need.'

However aggressive and unsatisfactory our exchange had been, at least it had been an exchange between two people, not just doctor and patient. She might break the tenuous transaction. I might ruin it by not being there when she wanted me or saying the wrong thing, but it was a start. It was a beginning and she'd got herself a job. Maybe, just maybe, she'd decide to give life a chance.

Mrs O'Halloran next. She was a pretty little woman who retained a country freshness in spite of the trauma of living with Ignatius and bearing his progeny. Mr O'Halloran was doing fine, she told me, confining himself to lemonade and attending daily Mass.

'And there's something else I've got to tell you, Doctor,' she added. 'You know I was thinking of having Everything Out. Well I haven't and I'm four months pregnant.'

I could only marvel at the victory of Ignatius's potency over his formidable ingestion of drink.

'Yes, I'm delighted.' She beamed. 'It'll be lovely to have a young one to run messages for us in our old age.'

As long as the messages weren't for beer, I was nearly going to say.

'And we've chosen a name for it, at least Mr O'Halloran has: Malachy if it's a boy and Petronella if it's a girl.'

I was just recovering from the impact of Mrs O'Halloran's optimism when Father Mortimer popped in. He looked ill and transparent but he wanted to tell me that the Abbot had been able to get Father Mason's case heard *in camera* and the priest was now on his way to a monastery in Wales.

'You look exhausted, Father,' I said. In fact he looked as if he was going to drop dead but he waved aside my offer of tea and said he was on his way to see a dying nun.

'Normally a most saintly little soul,' he said, 'and so plucky. But there's no accounting for human nature, is there, Doctor? When I brought her the Last Rites yesterday evening she rose up in the bed and said . . .' He could hardly bring out the words.

111

'She said quite clearly: "throw shit on the Pope" and then fell back in a coma.'

'No, there's no accounting, Father,' I said.

18

I'd had a trying morning. Mrs Lacey, the young woman whose GP said that she was haunting his surgery with aches and pains for which there was no organic foundation, was threatening to kill herself because she couldn't cope with four kids in a tiny flat. The flat was so small and insignificant that I couldn't find it on my map and I spent what seemed like half the morning careering around being misdirected by Irish navvies who, with the usual desire to please, didn't like to admit that they had no idea of where Dimsley Court was and so sent me right across the city and back several times.

When I did locate 10, Dimsley Court which was up three flights of dirty concrete stairs I understood poor Mrs Lacey's desperation. An infant, two toddlers and a snotty-nosed little boy of four were either yelling or moving remorselessly towards plugs and wires. A man, presumably Mr Lacey, lay in a chair with a paper over his face.

Mrs Lacey, red-eyed, her face puffy and with her hair tied back with a piece of string, attempted to control her flock like some wild and barbaric shepherdess.

'Sharon, come away from the balcony. Daren, put that cigarette out of your mouth. Oh Doc, I'm that glad you've come. I'm going out of my mind. It's this flat . . .'

I could see and hear what she meant. The rooms were tiny and cramped and the balcony was small, but any childish body could slip through and be pulped by the non-stop thundering traffic that made us all have to shout.

'I've asked and asked the Housing for a change but they don't want to know. Have you wet your knickers again, Shar?' She grabbed one child and patted the sodden bottom despairingly.

'And I'm that tired. What with him over there doing double

over-time and me working in a factory every morning I feel that done in. I don't know what I'd do if it wasn't for me Mum.'

Mr Lacey threw the paper from his lantern-jawed face and roared so loudly that the boy, Daren, set up a desolate howl.

'I've been sitting listening to you talking and it makes me want to vomit. Your Mum indeed. Nosey interfering old bag. We might be able to stick this lousy dump if it wasn't for her poking her hooter into everything. Tell the doctor about her. How she tells you to either have a sterilisation or get me to sleep on the settee. One of these days I'll bust her. I will that.'

'I can't help being soft. It's me nature.' Poor Mrs Lacey mopped her dripping nose with the baby's nappy.

'Soft? You're bloody putty in that rat-bag's hands. Well I've had enough. I'm working in a tannery when I should be doing welder's work, all to earn a bit more for you and the kids, and when I come home bushed, what do I find? My sodding mother-in-law poking her nose into our sex life.'

'Well, *your* mother spends most of the time in the pubs.'

'At least she doesn't interfere.'

I felt the helplessness I'd experienced with Ignatius O'Halloran, only this time it was worse. These people weren't psychiatric cases, they didn't need someone like me. They needed enough money to exist without poor beaten down Mrs Lacey going out to work and having to live in an inadequate flat near a mother who seemed to be stirring things up so that husband and wife viewed each other with hatred and despair.

'And they all come here,' he continued. 'Dr Lass going on about approaching the Housing when he knows they won't take a blind bit of notice 'cause we've already got a roof over our heads. And those young social workers that look like freaked-out junkies and the Health Visitor who says plenty but does nothing. And now you. Well, I'm sick of bloody doctors. Sick of them.'

I knew doctors weren't the most popular people but there was naked hatred and antagonism in Lacey's small fierce eyes and Mrs Lacey's sobbing was drowned by the non-stop thunder of the traffic outside.

'There's nothing mentally the matter with either of you,' I

said, trying to avoid the jammy fingers of one of the toddlers while Mrs Lacey clutched at the infant who was choking on his dummy. 'It's your circumstances . . .'

'Tell us something we don't know,' sneered Lacey. His face was streaked with sweat and dirt and, like his wife, he looked as if he hadn't slept for a week.

'Two things are clear to me,' I went on, 'and maybe I can help. You must get away from your in-laws and you must get a move from this flat. It's dangerous and quite unsuitable for children.'

'Yes. There was a child fell through the railings of the balcony only last week,' said Mrs Lacey.

I said I'd write a really slashing letter to the Housing. I'd state that if the family wasn't moved quickly to a house Mrs Lacey would certainly crack up and need hospitalization and that the children were in real and urgent danger from the balcony.

'And you can add that I'll have a breakdown meself if something isn't done,' Mr Lacey said. 'But Lass has tried to get us rehoused. Didn't even get a reply.'

I assured them that I'd do everything I could.

'I haven't told you about me back, Doctor.'

Mrs Lacey suddenly plunged the baby into my arms whilst she clutched the small of her thin back. I was conscious of a warm trickle seeping onto my lap through the threadbare nappy and then the ooze of something more pungent so I was relieved when the baby slid to the floor and began to gnaw at a stale biscuit.

Although Mr Lacey was a bit mollified by my obvious desire to help their miseries and Mrs Lacey wanted to get onto the subject of her dropped womb, it was getting on for two o'clock and my out-patient clinic patients would be waiting. I left the two Laceys festooned with their bawling offspring and clattered off down the stone steps. Behind me I could just hear poor Mrs Lacey yelling at her husband to turn on the TV even though it was some ancient Pinewood movie.

It was a clear crisp autumnal day and as I drove back to St Peter's I thought of the horrors of a life whose quality was reduced to watching some ageing movie star on such a lovely afternoon. But what else could they do? Where was there for the children to play? I rehearsed my sizzling phrases to the housing department which I'd dictate to Mrs Bell next morning. And to think that I'd always regarded Fidel and Che as revolutionary killers!

I'd hoped for an easy clinic because my bones ached, my eyes were gritty and I'd had nothing to eat since seven that morning, but I was mistaken. I was initiated into the new sport of 'doctor bashing'. I'd heard of it, I'd read about it, but I never actually experienced it till the Jordan family were shown in. Old Mrs Jordan, the mother, was a lollopy woman obviously tortured by her delusions and supported by a distressed-looking daughter-in-law and a son who thrust his mother at me and then collapsed into a chair covering his face with his hands.

'I want to go to the lav, but me bowels won't work. Take me to the lav. I want to go to the lav.' Mrs Jordan, swaying and lost, repeated her litany with rising intensity whilst her daughter-in-law tried to calm her in between telling me that Mother had already been before she came in and that she hadn't slept for a week and kept them all awake by making mooing sounds like a cow.

'We have to tie her in a chair or she'd turn up the gas. And she puts four dresses on if we don't watch her. The police are always bringing her back and the neighbours on both sides are always complaining. Something will have to be done. We can't go on.'

That was obvious. Poor Mrs Jordan was like a piece of moving protoplasm and in as much need of care and protection as one of the wild Lacey brood. But where could I put her? I had only one bed left and that was in a top ward which meant climbing three flights of stairs. Impossible with the state of poor Mrs Jordan's bolster-like legs and the panting of her strained heart.

I tried to get some information out of the old lady. Maybe there was a younger patient I could move. Or send someone on leave. My brain tried to compute urgent alternatives but I was tired and my ears rang with the old woman's repeated laments that her bowels were blocked. She stood wobbling and weeping and then young Mrs Jordan began to weep. I was going to suggest tea for us all when Mr Jordan, who had been sitting hunched over his folded arms, leaped to his feet and made a rush at me. Sister Bailey, the relief Sister who had just come in, paled.

'You get my mother a bed. Fast. Stop the cackle and get her a bed. I'm warning you. Get bloody cracking. I'm not leaving here till you get that bed. And after that I'm going to my MP, the Press and anyone who'll listen to me.'

I tried to say that that was exactly what I was doing, trying to find his mother a suitable bed, but I couldn't get the words out because of Jordan's ham-like fist clenched under my nose and the proximity of his purple face with saliva dribbling from his mouth. His wife flapped her hands helplessly. Sister moved forwards but Jordan shook her off and poor old Mrs Jordan went on about wanting to go to the lavatory.

'You fucking doctors,' Jordan said. 'We pay your bloody salaries, don't we? Us, the taxpayers, and what do we get when we want help? Nothing, bloody nothing.'

I rallied. My voice sounded far away but it was clear enough. I was aware of all my blood surging towards the lower part of my body and I had to hold on to the desk to stop my hand shaking.

'I'm trying to get your mother into a suitable bed but you're holding things up. If you don't calm now we're going to have to admit you as well with a coronary thrombosis.'

His cyanosis became less and he grew silent as if the maniacal fury which almost amounted to an epileptiform seizure had passed. Sister managed to coax the old woman to the door as I told her to take old Mrs Jordan to Parker ward and sort out a bed for her from there. Mr Jordan looked back at me as he shambled out waving his arms like a windmill as if making some sort of apologetic gesture. But he said nothing and slunk out after his demented parent.

'My God,' said Bailey, coming back with her apron twisted and her collar askew, 'we ought to get danger and dirt money.'

'I'll settle for some tea,' I said.

'I must say you handled that magnificently,' said Bailey. She was young and inexperienced and had only done two years as a sister but her praise was the perfect anodyne.

19

Next morning Mrs Bell was all solicitude about Mr Jordan's attack and I must say that when I looked back on the episode my own semi-composure surprised me, though what would have happened if he'd really bashed me I didn't know. I'd been lucky enough throughout my medical career about things like that. I'd had threats and letters like the 'I'm going to get you, Delaney,' one, once a patient had smacked me across my face and many were the flower pots and worse that I'd ducked in the old days. However, the dislike and hate of doctors I'd seen in Jordan's eye was something new and disturbing, but then, as Coulter said, the relatives of psychiatric patients were often dottier than the patients themselves and gnawed at by the guilt of rejecting them, so they transferred this on to nursing and medical staff.

I excelled myself in the sizzling letter I sent off to Treeview House, to the head of the housing department. I described the appallingly dangerous and unsuitable accommodation and the deplorable affect it was having on the Lacey household. Something must be done without delay or the Lacey parents would have to be admitted as patients and the children – those that had escaped the hazard of the balcony – would have to be placed in care, all of which would cost the ratepayers far more money than providing suitable accommodation. I ended by saying that it was remarkable to me as a doctor how the family had kept going without a major mishap but that this indeed was imminent if top priority and attention wasn't given to the Lacey's rehousing.

'You're really going to town, aren't you,' said Mrs Bell.

'And I'll keep chipping away till the housing people do something,' I said. 'I couldn't stick that hell-hole for a day, leave alone permanently.' I described to her the smell, the noise and the fraught condition of Mrs Lacey, with the children's nerves as taut as their parents' and having no place to play except a road that was a passport to a quick death.

Feeling I'd done what I could for the moment I asked Mrs Bell whether there had been any requests for domiciliary visits and she said yes, Miss Grieg, the matron of a home for the chronically sick called The Cedars, had phoned to ask me to visit. I liked Miss Grieg, a spinster Scot who ran the home with efficiency tempered with humanity. I wasn't so keen on Doctor Pond, the visiting GP who had so many irons in the fire that he never had time to tell you about his patients; Frankie said that that was because he didn't know anything about them.

I decided to go to The Cedars on my way home because it was on the same route, and after doing my letters I made my way to Parker ward. Lia was examining a patient on another ward but Logan was at her desk writing in the report book.

'Everything's quiet,' she said. 'It must be the moon.' Logan was of the generation of sisters, and there were still many, who put down all the patients' mood changes to the state of the moon.

'How's Sheena?' I asked.

'Up and dressed. I'll bring her along.'

When Sheena came to my clinic room she laughed at my expression. She had put on two stone and she exuded health and vitality. Gone were the suspicious looks and the air of fearful apprehension. She wore a white and red top over her black pants and her hair fell in a new rippling Rossetti style to her shoulders.

'And I'm off nearly all tablets except for the ones for the diabetes,' she said.

And that was nicely controlled, I saw on looking at her chart.

'And now I suppose you'll be wanting to go home?' I didn't quite believe that. Sheena was too bright not to know that she mustn't rush things.

'What I want first of all is to see Melinda, just to see her. And then later, when I've really got over this and found myself a place to live then I'd like to have Melinda back. They can't take her from me?'

'You mean adopt?'

'Yes.'

I said no, and tried to explain that Social Services having

119

'parental rights' was a temporary measure when the mother couldn't cope but that legally the child was Sheena's.

'I don't trust them.' Sheena spoke with the fear of one who has had experience of bureaucracy. She had been at their mercy too often. God, in her book, was always on the side of the heavy machines.

'I'll ring up Mrs Gibbons and ask her to take you to see Melinda,' I said. 'I'm sure she'll agree. I believe the couple who've got Melinda are very nice people.'

'But Melinda might forget me. I couldn't bear that.'

'I'll phone Mrs Gibbons now,' I said.

After Sheena went out I managed to get Mrs Gibbons on the phone. Yes, she'd heard Sheena was better and certainly she'd arrange for her to visit her daughter. I then sounded Mrs Gibbons out about the possibility of Sheena having her child back.

Mrs Gibbons' tone became guarded, still polite but evasive. Melinda was so happily placed with such good surrogate parents, wasn't it dangerous to expose the child to the limited care of a mother who had not just one but two serious illnesses?

'And I saw her when she was psychotic, Doctor, and she was really terrifying. Can't we leave this for some later date?'

'All Sheena is asking' I said, 'is not that she should have her child now; she knows she's not well enough and anyway she has no place to live. All she's asking is the promise that the return of Melinda will be considered at some stage?'

'You ought to know that promises depend on things like the patient's mental state and you can't guarantee that, can you, Doctor?'

'I can guarantee you that if Sheena hasn't the hope of ever having her child given back to her then she will end her life.' That was true, Sheena wouldn't make dramatic and unsuccessfull attempts at suicide like Joan Harris; she would turn her face to the wall and slip out of life.

'That may be so, Doctor, but one has to have regard for the interest of the child. Her care and welfare are of vital importance.'

I was beginning to dislike Mrs Gibbons.

'I'm aware of that,' I said. 'But there's never been any question of Sheena's ill-treating her child.'

'No, of course not,' Mrs Gibbons said, 'not by commission, but when she gets ill . . .'

'Look, lots of diabetics care for their children,' I said, 'and as regards the schizophrenia, well, it might never return.'

'And then again it might.'

Mrs Gibbons, possibly aware of the anger in my voice, said that why didn't she talk to her team leader, Mr Travis, and they could come down to Parker next week and have a meeting? She couldn't give any decision without the team and the team leader anyway.

That would be all right, I said and then had a brain-wave. I would of course, I said, advise Sheena to get herself a solicitor.

'Will that be necessary?' asked Mrs Gibbons somewhat huffily.

'I think so,' I said. 'You have her child . . .'

'Not permanently.'

'Then why can't you commit yourself more?'

'Well it has to be discussed by the team and the team leader . . .'

'Teams, team leaders. Like buses, you people seem to run in convoys,' I said. 'We're not in a relay race. OK. I'll set up the meeting.'

'Well of course I shall have to consult Mr Travis first to find out whether he can come. He's got so many commitments.'

The Cedars was a solid old house which a local merchant whose daughter suffered from polio had donated for the care of the chronically ill. The funds were ample enough for each patient to have a large bed-sitting room to himself and no expense had been spared with the furniture, curtaining or carpeting. In fact when you entered the wood-panelled hall with its antique chests and sombre oil paintings you felt you were in some Scots shooting lodge. Even Miss Grieg in her white veil and crisp piqué uniform and short red cape looked like a nursing sister in the First World War. It came as a shock when you saw the first wheel chair, the many patients walking with the aid of frames and calipers and the wasted limbs of the patients, mostly young, who couldn't move at all.

'Och, it's Pond getting the wind up.' Grieg made no secret of her lack of respect for Dr Pond – 'In and out like a flash of lightning and just as useless,' as she'd said once.

'This wee girl,' she went on, 'she's in her very early twenties. Annie Dent's her name. She was doing awfully well at University, reading biology or zoologoy or one of the "ologys" they do these days, when here she got a very bad multiple sclerosis . . . we used to call it disseminated sclerosis, do you remember?'

I did indeed. And I remembered how it struck down the young mostly and was a progressive destruction of all the sheaths covering the body nerves so that the patient's every function was affected, and in spite of remissions the end result was a paralysed incontinent patient. Because every nerve was affected at different times and in different ways the symptoms were insidious and the slurred speech, failing eyesight, transient pareses and bladder trouble were very often misdiagnosed until the malignant nature of the disease became all too evident.

'She's a grand wee girl, Annie,' Grieg said, leading me along the warm corridor towards the girl's room.

'And she's bound to get scunnered of the life in here. She's not close to her family who live in London and then her boy friend ditched her after she got ill. So she's had a rough time. The thing is, though, she's been sneaking out picking up men. Goes by taxi and of course old Pond's worried she'll get pregnant or worse. I must say from what you read in the papers Annie's running every danger of getting mugged or raped though she always takes off in a taxi.'

'But what can I do, Miss Grieg?' Poor kid, I was thinking, she's had a bad break already without me doing a Mrs Grundy act on her. I knew, of course, what Pond wanted. By involving me he'd be helping to keep himself in the clear if there was trouble, and he had a long sensitive nose for trouble.

'I think he thought a wee chat with you might help her. She might talk to you more freely. Here we are. May we come in, Annie dear?'

The room with its stereo equipment, French posters on the wall and books scattered everywhere could have been any young girl's room. And until the slender girl lying on the bed tried to get up you wouldn't realize that her gait was wobbly and that her arms and legs had a slight tremor. She had the pert, clean-scrubbed looks of an American girl, and when she smiled her teeth were very white against her tanned skin. She shook back her waist-length dark brown hair and pushed some red cushions behind her back to prop herself up.

'This is Dr Delaney, come to have a word with you, Annie. I'd better go and see what's happening to supper. That new cook's a devil with the salt when she's in bad humour, as she has been all week.'

'May I sit down, Annie?' I asked when Miss Grieg had gone off.

'Sure.' Annie reached over, the movement obviously causing her great effort, and shifted a huge Teddy bear from a chair beside her bed.

'That's Aristotle. I talk to him sometimes. Is that one of the first signs of dottiness?'

'I wouldn't have said you were dotty,' I said. 'And I gather the only reason they've asked me to see you is that you're worrying them by popping out without telling them.'

'Yes,' she said, taking up the Teddy bear and tweaking one of its ears. 'I buzz off in a taxi and have sex. D'you know what it's like being here day after day? Oh, they're good and kind, especially Miss Grieg, but it gets so bloody boring. I know I'm a cripple now but cripples still have urges, or didn't you know? Doctors seem to forget or ignore things like that. Especially old Pond who appears to think that my sexual organs have shrivelled up or something. When I asked him to put me on the Pill he nearly had a coronary.'

God knows, she had a right to be bitter, I thought, and it was unfortunate that Dr Piers Pond was the resident doctor. He was elderly and prudish and so rusty in his medicine that it was said that he still used poultices, bromides and other homely remedies common in the nineteen-twenties. He kept losing patients because he refused to supply the Pill but retained enough private patients who, lulled by his air of false and phoney confidence, stuck to him in sufficient numbers to help him own a Bentley. He also ran a lucrative private nursing home although the coroner had made some scathing remarks about some recent deaths there.

'It's like this,' Annie put down the bear. 'I had a boy friend at college. We had a good physical relationship. I enjoy sex but when I got this bloody MS, my bladder went funny and it put my boy friend off to . . . to have sex with a girl who has to have a catheter in her bladder now and again. Unaesthetic. So, he baled out did Bill. Well, at times I want sex so badly I'd have it with Aristotle if I could.'

'But isn't there anybody here of your own age?'

'Another patient?'

'Yes.'

'Have you seen them? The only blokes my age, and they're dears, I love them, but one of them has no feeling below his waist and the other can only move his head and neck muscles and has to be lifted everywhere by the nurses. Oh I'm the most active here I assure you.'

'It's just, if you could sort of tell Miss Grieg when you go out. So she won't worry so much.'

'Go and tell her I'm feeling randy and want a poke?'

'But can't you understand, Annie, how she feels? I mean, going with strange men. It's not the morals of it she's worried about, it's the danger.'

I knew that Grieg was broad minded because everyone knew she'd lived for years with a clergyman.

'Strange men?' Annie grinned broadly.

'Yes. You're bright. You know the perverts and kinks who are around? And it's not as if . . .'

I didn't know how to get around adding that it wasn't as if she was strong enough to defend herself, but she did it for me.

'Yes. I'm like a turtle. When I fall I can't pick myself up again. But I don't go with strange men.'

'Then who?'

'With Fred, the taxi driver. He's nice and clean and a surprisingly good lover. His wife is frigid and delighted to be left alone. And Fred's good to me. We do it in the back of the taxi in winter and in the park in summer.'

I burst out laughing and so did Annie.

'I was just thinking of the expression on Dr Pond's face if he knew,' I said. It was a most unethical thing to say but I didn't give a damn.

'Thank God you're not moralistic, rebuking or judging,' Annie said.

'Why should I be?' I asked. 'I don't think I'd do nearly as well as you if I got multiple sclerosis.'

And I meant it. Annie was gallant and brave and she was right about doctors pretending that invalids didn't or rather shouldn't have sex problems.

'Ah, but you wouldn't have a Fred,' she said. 'Will you come again and see me?'

'I'd like to. Is there anything at all I can do for you?'

'Yes. Get me a supply of the Pill,' she said. 'I'd adore to have a baby but I know it wouldn't be practical so I'll have to do with Aristotle.'

'I'll see you get a supply,' I said as Miss Grieg arrived.

Walking up the corridor I told her what Annie had said.

'Ah . . . Fred . . . I never thought of him to be sure. But he's an awfully nice chap. I might just provide them with a spare room when the weather gets cold.'

I couldn't be quite sure but I could have sworn Miss Grieg gave a wink.

20

The GP who phoned me about Mr Henry Maxton didn't bother
to go through Mrs Bell; he was a young and very bright doctor,
who made no secret of the fact that he was only waiting for his
visa for the States.

'I'm not going to be treated like shit for the next thirty years
and risk a coronary waiting for a pension that won't be worth
anything,' Tony Brick had said to me when I'd met him at a
dinner given by a drug company. He was thin and sharp-eyed
with a long nose and the air of an intelligent bird. He wasn't
liked by other doctors because he was so clever and had an un-
nerving habit of speaking his mind.

'This chap's mad in the good old-fashioned King Lear sense,'
he said to me. 'Mind you, the madness is quite well encapsulated
because he's teaching English at a local school and you don't realize how dotty he is till you get him on to the snakes.'

'The snakes?'

'Right,' Tony said. 'He looks sane, is well educated and quite
the gent, and he's managing to teach without anyone suspecting
the roaring inferno of insanity that's raging in his brain. He
thinks his house is infested with snakes, you see. I've been trying
to get him to see a psychiatrist for ages, but he's got no insight
and won't hear of it. Now I think he must. He's getting worse and
they're going to find out at school any day, and I don't want the
poor bloke to lose his job. I don't know what his norm is. He's a
bachelor and lives in a house on his own.'

'Where?' I asked, pen poised.

'This is too much, but it's true. He lives in number Six Nutley
Avenue, near Cuckoo Lane.'

God, this was nearly as bad as Benjamin and his Electric
Road, I thought, as I took down the address and said I'd visit that

very day.

'Make it after five, because he doesn't get home from school till near six,' Tony said. 'I must dash, going out to see another dotty devil who thinks he's being watched by golden Panda cars with Liberace type cops in them, but he's only dying to come in to you!'

'Where do you get them from, Tony?'

'Christ knows. I must have a heart like a marshmallow. Not like that bugger Coulter of yours. I tried to get him to take in a poor old duck who was dying and grossly demented, and he said he wasn't a magician and it wasn't in his brief to deal with geriatric cases.'

I said that I was a marshmallow too, and I wished I had some of Coulter's steel. Tony snapped back that that wasn't steel, just scrap metal, and sorry he had to go and could I phone him at evening surgery to let him know about Maxton?

It took me ages to get to Cuckoo Lane, which was situated in a very built-up part of the city at the very periphery of the catchment area. The evening was damp and the combination of the driving rain, whipped by wind against my dirty pane, which was made grimier by having more filthy water slashed against it every so often by the big lorries and trucks which lumbered by, was horrid. And Nutley Avenue wasn't evident on the map, so that it took me ages to locate the row of precise little houses with their neat gardens and respectably Victorian fronts. Number six was called "Joyville", although all I felt as I rang the bell was cold hunger.

The man who answered the door looked, as Tony had said, the perfect gent. His hair was snow white and his features commandingly majestic. Somehow, his brown complexion, which indicated his Eurasian extraction, made him more imposing, and he stood with regimental uprightness in a well-cut brown suit, cream shirt and green tie.

'Er . . . Dr Brick sent me,' I said. I couldn't think of what else to say. There was something most intimidating about Mr Maxton's stare.

'Have you come from the sanitation department, madam?'

'No,' I said.

127

'Really, that's rather remiss of Brick. He did promise to do something about this appalling business, you know. I'm rather disappointed. I thought he played with a straight bat.'

I had a brain-wave. I had come at Dr Brick's request I said, because he, Dr Brick, thought I might be able to help with, well with the 'appalling business.'

Mr Maxton's face unbent into a smile. His teeth were excellent and his skin was clear and tight against the good bone structure of his face. He'd be in his fifties, I'd judge.

'Are you an expert in reptiles then?'

No, I wasn't, I said, but I was anxious to help, and please would he let me in as I had come some distance and was cold and wet.

'Good heavens. Of course. Most kind of Dr Brick to send a lady like you whose time is so precious. *Do* come in.'

His tone became welcoming and mellow, and I recognized his type. He'd probably been born and educated in somewhere like Poona or Simla, father probably a railway clerk and mother a woman called Dolly or Tilly, whose early beauty had now deteriorated into a veiny bloatedness. But Henry would have been intelligent like most Eurasians and had 'got on'.

'Watch out,' he shouted, as I went into the dark little hall, which was very badly illuminated by one small ceiling light. 'Don't step in that spot. That's one of their battle marks. This way . . .'

He politely pushed me into a front room which was full of unopened parcels and cases. There were two trunks and I nearly fell over a pile of old newspapers on the floor.

'Do forgive me. Will you have a cup of tea?'

He nodded towards a table, cluttered with books and magazines, on which there was a teapot, some cups and a plate of stale looking Eccles cakes. Poor man, I thought, living alone and only kept going by his phobia. I said yes, I'd love a cup, and tried to swallow the tepid liquid, whilst refusing the ominous-looking cakes. The photographs on the wall showed a young and handsome Maxton, arm-in-arm with other young men, in what I supposed to be a sort of Indian 'chummery'. There were a few pictures of him in army uniform making a 'your country needs you' gesture, and several of young Maxton playing tennis and cricket. He looked like a brown-skinned Rupert Brooke.

'I don't think you've told me your name,' he said politely, offering me the milk.

I told him I was a doctor, not adding that I was a psychiatrist. I knew from experience that this could be an explosive admission!

He sipped his tea, sitting up very straight in the chair opposite me. He had thought I was a professional person, he said, and he apologized for his rudeness. But such was the harassment and strain he'd been subjected to by the reptilian invasion of his house over the past year, that his equanimity was being seriously disturbed. Had Dr Brick told me about the way snakes had taken over his dwelling?

'Yes, he told me about them, Mr Maxton,' I said, refusing another cup of tea. The stuff I'd drunk had left a strange lingering taste on my tongue, but I put it down to the fact that probably it was because Mr Maxton came from India and indulged in a special brand of tea.

'It is really getting unbearable.' Maxton jumped to his feet and pointed at a stain on the faded old carpet. 'Do you know what that is?' he demanded, pointing dramatically at it. I said no I didn't, and he said, 'That is snake's blood, and I should know. I was born and brought up in the tropics and I am familiar with snakes.'

'But where are they? I don't see any,' I said.

'Of course you don't. They only come out at night when there isn't anyone around. But one can hear them. Shish!'

He quivered like a pointer dog and held a hand to his ear. I told him I couldn't hear anything at all, and he said impatiently that that was what everyone said. He'd gone to the Police, the Sanitary Department and Dr Brick and he was getting very tired, weary and impatient with people's attitude of disbelief.

'Because the devils are breeding,' he told me, his eyes shining brightly and insanely. 'We shall be invaded by pythons, cobras, rattlers, and mambas. It was so bad last week that I couldn't sleep at all, and I lay on my bed with my shotgun by my side.'

I didn't like the sound of this at all, and wondered if Brick knew about the gun. I could see that Maxton's phobic delusion was fixed immovably, and quite unamenable to logic. He needed urgent admission to hospital for treatment, and I could only hope that he wouldn't be too difficult to persuade.

'But the worst danger of all,' he continued, 'the real terror, is the giant boa constrictor in the back room.'

'You mean there's a boa constrictor in the room behind us?'

'Definitely. A very nasty brute. Very nasty. He has a special smell. Can't you get it?'

I pretended to sniff. This man was very mad indeed, in the good old-fashioned, florid sense that made my mind boggle when I thought of how he coped with teaching. But probably, like many paranoids, he was only crazy when you got him on to the subject of his paranoia, and maybe he never mentioned snakes at school, having no occasion to do so.

I decided to make a last ditch attempt to ram some insight into Maxton. Could it be, I suggested, could it possibly be that he, Mr Maxton, having a vivid imagination, being brought up in India and living on his own, might imagine that there were snakes?

It was as if I'd accused him of rape, perjury and murder combined. He shot to his feet, made a salute and flushed a dusky pink brown.

'Are you suggesting that I am telling lies, madam?' he thundered.

No, no, I said, not at all, just that when people lived on their own and got a bit tense they sometimes . . .

He bit me off in mid-sentence, and told me that he never got tense. He'd taken a postal course in self-hypnosis and considered that he had no anxiety at all.

'As well as that, madam,' he drew himself up and sucked in his breath. 'As well as that, I would remind you that I have been a Scout Master and still observe the Scout's code of honour. Of course there are snakes here. I wish there were not, both for my own and for others' sakes, but there are and they must be dealt with.'

It was no good. The delusions were as fixed in his mind as if they'd been cemented there. But the incongruity of this soldierly-looking man in his neat little house, convinced that he was surrounded by dangerous reptiles, struck me as very bizarre.

It was approaching eight o'clock. This man must be got into

hospital as soon as possible. So, when he said that from the dubious look on my face he'd like to prove that the snakes really were there by showing me the boa constrictor in the back room, I said all right, I'd be interested to see it.

Then we must prepare ourselves, said Mr Maxton, leaping to his feet, and beginning to root in a cupboard. I said that I thought that this business of the snakes needed to be gone into. Mr Maxton agreed, and produced a dusty bottle of watery liquid. If he came into Barrington Hall, I went on, feeling hopeless and that he'd never take me up on the offer, if he came in for a rest I'd see to it that an investigation into the invasion of his house by snakes would be instigated.

'As it should have been a long time ago, madam. If that is the only way to do it then I will come in. I do need a rest. These snakes are affecting my sleep.'

I couldn't believe the cave-in. I had to reinforce it by asking him whether he'd come in that night?

'Yes. Yes,' said Mr Maxton rather impatiently. 'Now . . .'

He waved a rusty old sword he'd taken from the cupboard and handed me the bottle of liquid and a cloth.

'I shall go in front with the sword and you follow and be ready with the ether if I am attacked.'

This was crazy, I thought, clutching the bottle. But a whiff confirmed that it was indeed ether. Suppose Maxton, overcome by some fresh delusion, rammed it over my face? Or, worst fear of all, suppose there really was a snake in the back room!

If anyone saw me padding after this large man brandishing his old sword like a crazy Quixote, and carrying a bottle of ether with a view to anaesthetizing a boa constrictor, they'd wonder about *my* sanity.

'Quietly, quietly.' Mr Maxton padded in front of me through the murky little hall, and bent down to deal with the intricate locks on the back-room door. I felt more than a frisson of fear when he opened the door very, very slowly, but I made myself follow him into the back room, which was crammed with old carpets rolled up, dusty furniture and more piles of books, journals and magazines. It seemed as if Mr Maxton had lived here for years and had never unpacked.

'Come out, come out,' Mr Maxton called, and for a ghastly moment I thought I heard a slithering sound.

We waited ten minutes, and I asked where the snake was? Maxton wasn't in the least put out.

'Gone to ground. They're cunning devils, as I told you. Oh, well. That's it then. I'd better come with you and try and get a night's sleep. As long as they don't find out where I have gone to. Then we are all undone.'

Mr Maxton came into hospital and started a course of injections which were so successful that, when I met him taking a walk in the hospital grounds two weeks later, I stopped, smiled and asked him how he was?

'In excellent health,' he said, 'but then I always have enjoyed good health.'

I gently tried to ascertain whether he remembered me?

'I've never had the pleasure of meeting you,' he said. 'It may have been my brother Maurice. We are very alike and are often mistaken for each other.'

Mr Hood reported that Mr Maxton never mentioned snakes, and after beating everyone at chess, he left hospital and returned to work.

21

Mrs Gibbons rang me up to say that she and Mr Travis would be able to come down for a meeting on Sheena next Tuesday, which was a week from today, and would that be all right for me?

I said yes, I'd nothing lined up for that day except for some visits in the morning. Actually everything was very quiet in the hospital and I took advantage of the lull to find out how Sheena was doing in her search for accommodation of some sort.

She was having no luck, in spite of help from the nursing staff, friends of the hospital and her own acquaintances. Nothing suitable had been found and in spite of the girl's brave front I was worried that this continued waiting might pressurize her into another attack of psychosis. But maybe Mrs Gibbons and Mr Travis would be able to help. I pinned my hopes to that and tried to cheer up Sheena.

My mind was taken off Sheena and her troubles by a frantic call from a social worker called Miss Bolt who said that a mad and very drunken mother called Mrs Nelligan had turned up demanding to take her small son Peter from school.

'I know Chrissie,' said Miss Bolt. 'The department has had trouble with her and her family for years. She herself has been a patient in Barrington Hall, she drinks, and has two other children by a West Indian and a Pakistani. The school is over for the day but the teachers are frightened of letting Chrissie have Peter who's been in the charge of Miss Kyle, one of our workers.'

'Is Chrissie needing admission?' I asked.

'In my opinion, yes. At the moment she's managed to get herself up into one of the first floor classrooms and is standing in front of a large window waving a broken barley wine bottle and threatening to "do" anyone who comes near her. We can't locate her GP, he's probably out on visits, but we'd like you to come.

The school's in Corporation Avenue.'

'I know it,' I said. The school was even more dilapidated than St Bede's and situated in a very tough area indeed. And I was beginning to remember Chrissie, an agressive Glaswegian whose manic depressive condition was not helped by her frequent binges on barley wine.

I didn't like the sound of this at all and I liked it less when I drove through the crowds gathered about the school gates staring up at a window on the first floor where the wild figure of Chrissie was clearly outlined.

'Thank goodness you've come, doctor.' Mr Dane, the head teacher, was a mild man who looked as if he had ulcers and two young male teachers standing beside him seemed frankly terrified.

'I don't know how she got up the stairs and into the classroom but she's there and she's standing in front of the big window in — well — what I'd call a maniacal state. What are we going to do? She could go through the window at any moment. And she's threatening to assault anyone who goes near her. It's really terrible.'

'Think of your ulcers,' said a motherly looking woman who seemed to be an assistant teacher.

'Look, I'll have to try and talk to her,' I decided. I sounded most intrepid but I felt a bit quivery inside. Fortunately Miss Bolt, who looked a determined and resourceful girl, said that the main thing was that the child Peter was safe in another part of the building and that she would telephone Barrington Hall and say that a very disturbed patient was on her way and would they send the ambulance immediately?

'How long will it take? Just listen to her,' Mr Dane moaned and loosened his tie. The motherly teacher patted him soothingly on the shoulder and the two young male teachers tried to look as if they were equal to any situation.

The hoarse roars of Chrissie could be heard from upstairs and one of the male teachers said: 'Are you suggesting that she's to be forced to come into hospital? Surely she could be persuaded . . .'

Miss Bolt looked to the ceiling and I said, 'I'm afraid you don't know Chrissie.'

Miss Bolt went off to phone the hospital and I picked up my black bag and asked who would come up to beard Chrissie with me?

'Please forgive me.' Poor Mr Dane looked on the verge of collapse. 'My health is very poor and we've just been in the papers over a case of bullying and now this.'

After a steely look from Mrs Plum, the matronly looking teacher, the two young men, Mr Apley and Mr Gordon, said that they didn't mind coming up with me. Their pale faces and sweaty foreheads belied this but as we climbed the stairs towards the classroom from which Chrissie was bellowing, Mr Apley, a slim young man with a rather pixie-like fragility, seemed to summon up courage from somewhere and said wasn't this a job for the police and should he phone them?

'It may well be a job for the police,' I said, 'but I think you'll find that when they hear Mrs Nelligan is an ex-patient of Barrington Hall they'll be only too pleased to hand her over to us. She does need psychiatric help anyway.'

'Poor little lad, her son,' Apley said. 'I was always worried about those bruise marks he had on his legs and arms.'

Then why the hell didn't you report them, I nearly said, but our words were drowned by the shrieks of Mrs Nelligan who was standing, legs straddled, in front of a large glass window which looked out over the yard in front of the school. People were gazing up with the half ashamed anticipation of something gruesome and bloody about to happen.

I only dimly noticed the desks, the blackboard and the old remembered smell of ink, rubber and body heat. Chrissie transfixed my attention. She stood waving her broken bottle of barley wine and her sleazy old clothes hung on her skinny body. Her hair was a wild bush of carrot red against a face that was naturally pale but made more so by malnutrition, and there were sores around her mouth. But her voice, with its hard Glaswegian accent, was clear and explicit. 'You come near me, you bastards, and the first one of ye will get this full in the face. Now, I'm no telling lies. Ahm tellin' the truth.'

And I believed her. I didn't know how drunk she was but I remembered what she'd been like when she'd been in hospital –

so violent she'd had to have massive daily doses of drugs and she'd thrown a chair at a patient and tried to throttle a nurse. But she'd settled with treatment. Probably now she hadn't bothered with her treatment and had obviously been neglecting herself.

'Do you remember me, Chrissie?' I asked.

'I'm no that daft,' she said. 'But you'll not get me back to that bloody loony bin. Definitely not. Where's ma kid? Where's wee Peter?'

'He's safe,' I said. 'You don't look well, Chris. Who are you living with now? Last time you were happy enough with Pete.'

'Aye, Peter's father. The bugger went off with another girl and I took up with this friggin' Paki and I'm no tellin' you a lie but he's a king of the bastards. Look. . . .'

She pulled up her threadbare dress sleeves and bruises were clearly visible. 'And he bashes Peter, too. I'm away back to Dundee I am, and that sodding Paki can make his own curry.'

'You're not well enough yet, Chrissie,' I said. 'Why not have a rest in hospital and when you're well then you can make plans?'

'I want ma kid.' She swayed and I knew she was getting exhausted from booze, lack of food and the continual shouting.

'The ambulance has arrived and everything's ready.'

Miss Bolt had appeared beside me whilst Mr Dane propped up by his motherly colleague tottered up to me and said, 'Why can't you get her out? I don't like this at all, Doctor. There's more people collecting. I thought that there were drugs and things you could give these days . . .'

I nearly said that it would mean shooting a dart containing a sedative drug to hit the bellowing Chrissie when Miss Bolt threw me a sympathetic look and said that she didn't mind approaching Chrissie with me. The only way we could prevent her from throwing herself out of the window was to get close to her and that meant risking the jagged edged bottle being smashed in one or both of our faces.

'Nasty one this,' said one of the two huge ambulancemen who had appeared. 'She looks dangerous.'

I felt like saying 'Only when she bites', as had been said to me about the paranoid woman's yapping Alsatian who had made a leap at me, but I knew that there was only one thing to do. To get to Chrissie and to get some sedative drugs into her. And fast. Her shouting was growing louder again and her threats more malevolent.

'I'll bust any fucker that comes at me. I'm beaten by that bloody Paki. He tells me to go on the streets to earn money and now you're going to take wee Peter. Well I'm tellin' ye I'll do for yez all . . .'

'Come on,' I said. I had already filled a syringe with some Largactil, and although I dreaded advancing towards this dangerous drunken woman I knew that there was nothing else to be done.

With Miss Bolt beside me and the two male teachers rather falteringly bringing up the rear we moved towards Chrissie.

'I'm tellin' ye,' she screamed. 'Now I'm tellin' ye that the first one tries to get me is going to get this bottle right in the kisser.'

I could feel the smash of the bottle on my face, the tearing out of an eye maybe. It was a long time since I'd seen a gouged-out eye but I remembered it from Casualty. And the warm trickle of blood blinding the real injuries. I was in a dream. A sick nightmare where my limbs liquefied, and although the monsters were approaching my boneless limbs were powerless to get me to my feet, leave alone run.

'You're very tired, Chrissie,' I said, and flicked an eye at Miss Bolt, muttering from the side of my mouth for her, Miss Bolt, to grab the bottle if she could, while I kept Chrissie talking.

'I'm no that tired.' Chrissie was very hoarse now and she had difficulty keeping herself upright. 'I've nothing against you but I've been beaten so much I don't know whether I'm coming or going.'

'Come in to us for a bit, Chrissie,' I said.

'But where's ma wee Peter?'

'He's being looked after.'

'Well, if I go can I see him for a wee bit? Just to say good bye?'

The shouting had stopped and she looked what she was, a poor, beaten-down semi-drunken drab. But I couldn't risk her child seeing her like that and I said no, she couldn't see him now but when she came out . . . She gave a piercing yell and Miss Bolt was just in time to snatch the broken bottle before it came flying at me.

There was no more fight left in her. She was too tired and too hungry and too ravaged by the effects of her drink. She slid to the floor and said wearily, 'Aye, all right. I'll come with you. But look after wee Peter.'

She didn't need an injection after all. Her eyelids were fluttering in the sleep she sorely needed, and Miss Bolt and myself were able to help her towards the ambulancemen who were waiting with a stretcher.

'Mind you,' said one, the larger one, 'I wouldn't touch her if she'd refused to go. You have to remember the dignity of the individual. And the danger. Why, a man bit me on the calf last year.'

I felt a distinct urge to bite him myself, but it was only the aftermath of trying to deal with danger, and I was saved from making a reply I'd afterwards regret by an invitation to tea in the staff room as Chrissie was led away to the ambulance.

'Terrible thing to happen,' Mr Dane said, his face blue-white as we were drinking our tea. 'I don't like these sort of things at all. I really don't know how you do this sort of job, Doctor. So sordid. Mind you, things have got to such a pass in the teaching world that I'm getting out in six months, but I don't think I can ever remember anything as bad as this. Barley wine and Pakistanis! Women degrade themselves so.'

Miss Bolt and I just looked at each other. After all, what was there to say?

22

I called at Garland House to cheer myself up after the Chrissie
Nelligan episode only to find Barney in bed and Frankie steeped
in gloom but as usual taking out her depression in activity, this
time dashing away at a sewing machine making a gloriously
coloured flamingo pink kaftan.

'Nothing but trouble,' she said before I could tell her about
Chrissie.

'Old Sullivan's dead. Fell down a manhole, stupefied with
booze, I suppose. Anyway, Barney's taken it badly. Especially as
Willy isn't well either.'

She nodded to where Willy was sprawled, wheezing in his
basket by the fire.

'Christ, it's like telepathy between that animal and Barney,'
she said, snipping off thread with her teeth, 'like a bloody
couvade.'

There was a sepulchral moan from upstairs and the quavering
tones of Barney.

'I think I'm having a rigor. Bring me an aspirin or something
for God's sake.'

'The one that's supposed to be deaf,' sniffed Frankie, opening
her bag and getting an aspirin from the packet she'd taken out.
'Why, he's got ears like a dog,' she added as she went into the kitchen for a glass of water. 'Come on, let's go up to him.'

Willy lumbered after us but gave up half way, slumping back
on the hearth rug.

I'd witnessed Barney's remarkable ability to look *in extremis*
before, but this time his appearance really disturbed me. His normally round face had shrivelled and even his perky white moustache drooped sadly. And I'd never seen him without his toupé.
He looked like a very old and ill baby.

'I've had a great blow in losing Jerry Sullivan,' he said to me, cramming the tablets Frankie handed him into his mouth and then gulping water. 'My last link with life gone. Nothing left now.'

Tears rolled down his flaccid cheeks and old Willy, having at last heaved himself up the stairs, stood by Barney's bed. Barney, made more emotional by the appearance of his dog, patted the animal with a purple veined hand.

'No, nothing to live for,' he wailed.

This was either a *tour de force* of his acting ability or a dramatic indication of how he really felt. I suspected that it was a bit of both, and I could see that even Frankie was affected as she tried to rearrange the pile of blankets and sheets that Barney's thrashing limbs had thrown into chaos.

'You've got me, haven't you?' she shouted into Barney's so-called good ear.

'What's that? What are you saying? That's another thing. I'm getting deafer every bloody day.'

'I'm telling you that you have me,' Frankie tried again.

Barney allowed himself a grimly cynical smile. 'Oh, yes. So you say. So you say. But you'll get tired and bored of me, and I don't want pity.'

I thought he was going to launch into his 'Finish me off' monologue but Frankie, controlling herself admirably, told Barney that he was bound to feel upset about losing his old friend, and that after all Sullivan hadn't suffered.

'No. That's it. I envy the bugger. Used to love his grub, you know, and always said he'd like to die eating. Well this is the next best thing. Quick and sudden. Jesus, what a bloody life. And yet some stupid sods tell you that there's a God.'

'Would you like a brandy?' Frankie asked loudly, and Barney raising himself shakily asked, 'Candy? What the fucking hell would I need candy for? Unless you're going to add cyanide!'

'She means brandy,' I yelled in his ear. He nodded weakly and on the way down I asked Frankie whether, in view of Barney's wraith-like appearance, we shouldn't call Cousins in.

'I'll wait till tomorrow. You know the Osborn powers of recovery.'

'And get some sleep yourself,' I said. She looked pallid and drawn, her skin pasty and the normally curly hair was hanging around her face in witch's straggles.

'Ah . . . he'll see me off before he goes,' she said at the door.

When I phoned next morning, as predicted, Barney was up and dressed after a good breakfast and had even gone out on business.

'Don't know what it is,' Frankie said. 'You know how secretive Barney can be. But it's something about Sullivan. Something about the will.'

I was cut off from saying that that might bode well for Barney when Logan came in to announce that Mr Travis, Mrs Gibbons and a Miss Ingleside from Social Services had arrived.

Travis was a big bear-like man. He had a kind, tired face and looked like someone's uncle. Mrs Gibbons was a cheerful blonde in early middle age and Miss Ingleside was tall and young, her clever face hidden by falls of long hair and Granny glasses.

'Well, we're all busy people.' Travis glanced at the folders we all carried and his own bulging brief case. 'So there's really no need for me to go into great detail about Sheena Boden, is there? It's really a very sad and tragic case. Here we have a young girl, with no relatives and a husband who can't be traced, stricken down by two serious illnesses . . .'

'Now in abeyance,' I said quickly.

'But nevertheless you'd agree that at any time one or the other could flare up, wouldn't you, Doctor?' Travis was kind but persistent.

'Unlikely with the present-day treatment for both diseases,' I said. 'Now if she had multiple sclerosis or something like that . . .'

'Still, we are dealing with an unhealthy and vulnerable girl. Now I think that again we all agree that the child Melinda's welfare must come first.'

'Surely the child's and the mother's welfare are interconnected,' I said.

Travis didn't comment but went on. 'At the moment Melinda is happily placed with foster-parents, well known to us for their kindness to children. The child is happy and well adjusted. Are

141

we to expose her to the trauma of a mother who, with the best of intentions, simply cannot give her the care that these foster parents give her?'

'Sheena was delighted at how well Melinda looked when I took her to see her,' Mrs Gibbons said. She had a pleasant beaming face and Travis was obviously well disposed to her. Miss Ingleside, whose function seemed to be that of a student, said nothing but kept writing rapidly in a notebook.

'I've no doubt that the foster parents are looking after Melinda very well,' I said. 'But as well as "care" there's also the question of the "love" which only Sheena can give the child. Melinda needs that and I'm sure that she'll be an enormous help and support to Sheena.'

Silence. Travis riffled through his notes, Mrs Gibbons looked benign and Miss Ingleside retrieved her *New Society* which had fallen out of her bag.

'You see,' Travis went on, his voice careful and measured as if he was speaking to aborigines, 'there's no question of adoption . . . well . . . not yet. We, the department, have assumed parental rights over Melinda which does not mean that we've taken the child away from Sheena in law but are just acting as the child's parents until such time as Sheena herself can resume her parental rule.'

'But that's just what she's terrified of,' I said. 'She thinks that you're always going to have "parental rights".'

'Dear me, no,' Mrs Gibbons smiled, 'it's a purely temporary thing. Purely temporary. I think that we, in the caring professions, are all motivated by anxiety to do what is best for parent and child. In this case we have a happily settled child and a mother who, with all the love in the world, can't look after that child.'

'But this is the point,' I said, 'the girl is worried sick about not being able to find a place to live and not getting a clear assurance that her child won't be taken away from her permanently. How can she look after the child when she has nowhere to live?

'Has she tried?' asked Mrs Gibbons. 'You see, Doctor, I'm concerned to see how Sheena is going to function when she leaves the protective environment of the hospital. In other words, she's got to *prove* herself.'

I could feel a slow burning anger coming over me. There they all sat, kind, well-meaning people but so hamstrung by the red tape of bureaucracy that the human factor had disappeared.

'How can she prove herself if she doesn't get a chance to?' I asked. 'It's a real double bind situation, isn't it? She's bright, she knows she can't have her child for a long time. What she's asking, and what I want to know, is whether, when she gets a home together, she may be able to have Melinda back?'

'We really can't commit ourselves to anything definite until this girl, who unfortunately has such an unstable history, has shown that she can manage in the community.'

'Then, would you tell Sheena this, she's waiting outside?' I said, getting up. Mrs Gibbons looked uncomfortable and Travis asked whether it would be really necessary and couldn't I explain things to the girl?

'Doctor,' Travis passed a hand over his forehead. He looked as if he might have a migraine, 'I don't want this to be acrimonious. We deeply sympathize with this poor girl but you must remember that we see a horrifying amount of child neglect and cruelty cases and we have to be very careful.'

I said that yes, I understood that but Sheena, he must remember, wasn't asking for her child back right away.

'But let her explain herself,' I said.

Sheena came in, looking pale but composed. Mr Travis gently went over more or less what he'd said to me. Melinda was being well cared for and didn't Sheena think the child was best left where she was while she, Sheena, was ill?

'But I'm not ill now,' Sheena said. 'And I don't want to have Melinda back right away. I'm prepared to wait. For a year even. But what I want is for you to tell me that there is the hope that one day I'll have my daughter back.'

'Now you can't pin us down too much, Sheena,' Mrs Gibbons said. 'You'll have to find somewhere to live after all and show us that you can manage outside . . .'

'I've been trying to find a place,' said Sheena. 'Can you help me?'

'It's frightfully difficult around this area,' Travis said, 'and you'd have to wait a terribly long time, I'm afraid.'

'Then how can I "prove" myself?' asked poor Sheena. 'But I'm telling you . . . as I told my solicitor. . . .'

'A solicitor?' Travis didn't look pleased. 'Don't you trust us, Sheena?'

'I want my child back some day,' said Sheena. 'I want you to tell me that I haven't lost my rights to my child.'

Mrs Gibbons used her soothing tone. 'Our assumption of parental rights is purely temporary, as we've told you.'

'But you haven't said that there's the possibility of my having my child back,' she said obstinately. I didn't know she had such guts.

I couldn't stop myself from butting in here. Sheena had been an excellent and co-operative patient, I stated. She was willing to live near the hospital so that we could keep a strict eye on her. She wasn't demanding her daughter back right away, merely an assurance that the case would be reassessed when she got established.

I made it all sound so easy, Travis smiled tiredly. If I knew how busy their department was, the number of patients in worse plights than Sheena, the amount of abandoned, neglected and ill-treated young people that they had to deal with daily, then perhaps I wouldn't be tempted to, he had to say it, 'oversimplify' the issues.

'You tell me my child isn't adopted,' Sheena broke in, 'won't be adopted, without my consent and that she has to remain with foster parents until I can provide suitable accommodation, a home in fact for us both, and yet you can't help me find accommodation.'

'Let's not get too emotional,' Travis said.

And Sheena flashed, 'If it was your kid you would. Well, after this morning I realize that I need my solicitor more than ever and I hope he'll be able to make the right noises because I'm never going to give Melinda up, never, ever.'

She walked out and Travis sighed and looked at his watch. He had to visit two problem families and Mrs Gibbons was going on to interview a mother who was supposed to have flung her child across the room causing a brain haemorrhage.

Well-intentioned good people, I thought, as I watched them go, but I agreed with Sheena. She was a butterfly caught on the wheel of bureaucracy and she needed her solicitor. Besides, it wasn't just Melinda she was fighting for, it was her life. With Melinda taken from her there was nothing to live for and this morning she hadn't even been given the hope that she so desperately needed.

23

Time sneaked up on me. Jack Duggan was due back in ten days' time and then I'd be relegated to what Frankie called medical stooging. But worse than that; nothing more had been done for Sheena and, knowing Jack as I did, I was pretty certain he'd want to do a good 'clean out' of my patients to rattle up some business with the GPs. He'd need empty beds and Sheena would find herself placed in some hostel or home where it would be impossible for her to establish a nest for herself and her child.

As usual I decided to consult Frankie and Barney who were both more or less restored to their precarious state of equilibrium. Frankie answered the phone and said that Barney seemed to have got over Sullivan's death and was giving all his attention to Willy who had apparently developed some obscure canine complaint. But her soft heart was touched when she heard about Sheena and the lack of progress we seemed to be making with her.

'And when Jack the Ripper gets back that'll be poor Sheena given the order of the boot,' she said.

'Only she'll then come back in a schizophrenic relapse which may become chronic,' I said.

'You know, we've got that basement flat,' Frankie said, 'and we're so bloody hard up we were going to let it, but after two Nigerians and a bloke and his boy friend from Iraq applied for it Barney said, the hell with it. Listen, Sir is waving to me about something. He's just come from the vet's and from the colour of his face he's had a few jars on the way home. Yes . . . I'm coming.' Before ringing off she told me insistently to come down to see them the following night.

I knew that something momentous had happened when Frankie greeted me the next evening. Her impressively coiled hair style would have been most majestic if she hadn't applied her lipstick with such dashing enthusiasm and, judging from the powerful exudation of 'Ma Griffe' from her person, she must have doused herself with half of what I knew to be her last precious bottle. Mind you, Willy, sulky but evidently healthy, had a very nasty smell so perhaps Frankie's lavish use of scent was necessary.

As for Barney, he looked magnificent in a navy pin-stripe suit and red bow tie and he walked and talked in such a regimental way that I knew he had had a lot to drink. For all the liquor that went down the Osborn gullet I'd never seen him drunk. If he had a load on, it only made him extra cautious, like now.

'Our dear friend, through all our vicissitudes.' He gave me a smacking kiss on both cheeks and indicated an amazing array of drinks in a grandiloquently Micawberish way. 'Champagne. It must be champagne.'

As he opened a bottle of Dom Perignon with flourishing panache Frankie tried to shoo Willy outside and Barney commanded. 'Leave the poor beast be.'

'But the smell Barney . . . it's horrible . . .'

'Smell or no smell, Willy is our friend, like Joyce. And shall share in our rejocing.'

He handed me a tulip glass of champagne and poured more for Frankie and himself.

What the hell was it all about? I asked. I hadn't seen the pair of them so elated since Barney had won a Tote double two years ago. 'What's happened?' I asked, and Barney refilled my glass before I'd had time to empty it.

'The most marvellous thing,' broke in Frankie. 'You'll never believe it, Joyce. I always thought that you and me and Barney would end our days selling matches but yesterday morning we heard great news.'

'Most welcome. And generous. But not entirely unexpected.' Barney stood in front of the fireplace. He looked rosy and happy and all of a piece and I wondered, as I'd wondered many and many a time, at his powerful recuperative powers.

'I won't keep you in agony Joyce.' Frankie waved her champagne glass triumphantly. 'The fact is that old Sullivan has left us a legacy.'

'The will still has to go through Probate but I understand it's a tidy sum. A tidy sum.' Barney twirled his white moustache with Edwardian gusto.

'Oh, for Christ's sake don't be so secretive, tell her how much. Seventy-five thousand pounds, that's how much Joyce.'

I was flabbergasted. Frankie and Barney were both hopeless with what little money they had and I knew myself that there were an awful lot of bums and down-and-outs who'd touched Frankie for money that was never returned.

'We can have a really long holiday in the Seychelles now. And I'll get a sable coat. Not mink. I've always wanted sable. And a big common diamond ring as big as the Ritz.'

'Easy, easy, Frankie, you're forgetting inflation,' Barney said. 'I shall have to have a long talk with my stockbroker. Perhaps he'll show me a bit more respect now.'

'And for you Joyce . . . What would you like? A fur coat? A holiday? Come on, tell me, remember the time you kept me for six months after I was all to pieces when Benny was taken into St Pats with the DT.'

The champagne was too much for Frankie; and Barney – well lubricated for a fight – was ready to take her up on Benny who'd been the alcoholic lawyer with whom Frankie had been in love many years ago. Then I thought of something to distract them.

'Frankie,' I said, 'did you mean it about letting Sheena have the basement flat here? Or have you different plans now, moving house or what?'

'What the hell's this?' Barney demanded. 'You're always bloody well doing things behind my back. What's this?'

'Things haven't changed at all,' Frankie said. She wasn't drunk. She was euphoric more than inebriated. 'I was only joking about diamonds and minks and sables. But not about the Seychelles. Listen, Barney. . . .'

Patiently she told Barney about Sheena and her troubles and I could see that he was moved. His heart, like her own, was tender, especially about young people and animals. He'd been brought up in a home himself and he always felt for parentless children.

'She's a quiet, pleasant girl. The child's a pet and she'd be very useful helping with the cooking and being in the house when I'm out,' Frankie said. 'So what do you say Barney?'

'I say yes. Poor kid. The buggers can't take her child from her. Of course she can come here. One thing though . . . will she get on with Willy?'

We both said yes of course she would and Barney refilled our glasses and launched into a eulogy of old Jeremiah Sullivan. After two bottles of champagne Barney winked and said knowingly, 'Course there was a time when I got him out of a damn awkward spot in Simla. He was courting a Miss Patch. . . yes, that was her name, Prudence Patch and Christ she looked it. Anyway old Sullivan goes and gets himself a dose of clap from a very pretty Eurasian girl called Trixie. Yes, that was her name, damned if I can think of her second name. But she was a peach was Trixie. Course old Sullivan nearly went demented but I fixed him up,' Barney closed a rather bloodshot eye. 'I got him fixed up. Sick leave and all. Though he never did marry that Patch woman.'

'Well here's to clap if this is what it gets you,' Frankie laughed, waving her glass, and Barney told her not to be coarse, at the same time grinning widely.

I told them I'd ask Sheena about the flat in the morning, and even allowing for the benignity induced by the champagne I knew they'd both keep to their word.

I sent for Sheena next morning and put it to her. Would she like to try living in Dr Mullen's flat and then if she made out all right she could apply to have Melinda.

'You know Dr Mullen, Sheena?' I said. 'And of course she has a companion, Major Osborn, with whom she lives? Now, they argue a little at times but they're kind people and I think it would be a good thing for you. It's a start.'

'It's more, Doctor,' she said. 'It's hope. Thank you very much. When can I go?'

I said I'd see Sister, and as I waited for Logan I thought of everything that could go wrong. Barney could be insufferable. After all, we were used to him. And Frankie was erratic. Willy mightn't like the child.

The solution for Sheena seemed too good to be true but the

stakes were worth the gamble. How difficult life was, I ruminated.

'You look as if you're seeing a vision, Doctor,' said Sister Logan when she brought in the tea. And I was but I didn't tell her what it was.

I was seeing the elongated figure of Mother Aloysius, the Reverend Mother of my convent school, shaking her long pointed finger and reminding me that life was more than just lying in an armchair with a book and a box of chocolates at my elbow.

How right she was!

AND IF YOU'VE ENJOYED THIS BOOK
WHY NOT READ . . .

JUST HERE, DOCTOR

DR ROBERT CLIFFORD

JUST HERE, DOCTOR is the true story of a young
country doctor and his patients – a richly entertaining
and humorous chronicle of the life of a small West
Country community as seen through the eyes of its G.P.

Dr Clifford has some marvellous stories to tell: about
the home delivery of a cricket fan's baby – in between
overs of a televised Test Match . . . of the time he rode off
on a gigantic horse to attend a hunting casualty – and rode
back in an ambulance *as* the casualty . . . and the amazing
saga of his student rugby tour of France – the craziest,
most drunken ever undertaken. Here too, on the more
serious side, are moving accounts of the courage of
ordinary people in the face of serious, even fatal, illness.

The author has written a book teeming with colourful and
curious places and characters, packed with comedy, drama
and tragedy.

0 7221 0483 9   85p

BIOGRAPHY

WITHOUT FEATHERS

WOODY ALLEN

Woody Allen's guide to coping with what life has to offer –
from finding excuses for psychic phenomena to the mysteries
of Mensa, from God (or lack of God) to a brief, yet
helpful, guide to civil disobedience. This is Woody Allen
at his hilarious best – a genius in the tradition of Groucho
Marx and James Thurber. A man whose simple artistic
ambition is 'to forge in the smithy of my soul the un-
created conscience of my race. And then to see if I can
get them mass-produced in plastic'.

'Allen is as skilful as any humorous writer of the last
thirty years' *The Spectator*

'It will get you giggling deep down' *The Observer*

0 7221 1114 2 95p

HUMOUR

Book Tokens

**Give them
the pleasure of choosing**

Book Tokens can be bought
and exchanged at most
bookshops.

A selection of bestsellers from SPHERE

Fiction

REVENGE OF THE MANITOU	Graham Masterton	£1.10	☐
SHARKY'S MACHINE	William Diehl	£1.50	☐
WAR STORY	Gordon McGill	£1.00	☐
FIRE STORM	Robert L. Duncan	£1.10	☐
THE GLENDOWER LEGACY	Thomas Gifford	£1.25	☐

Film and TV Tie-ins

SATURN 3	Steve Gallagher	95p	☐
DAWN OF THE DEAD (filmed as ZOMBIES)			
	George Romero & Suzannah Sparrow	85p	☐
THE PROMISE	Danielle Steel	95p	☐
THE PROFESSIONALS 7: HIDING TO NOTHING			
	Ken Blake	85p	☐
THE PROFESSIONALS 8: DEAD RECKONING			
	Ken Blake	85p	☐

Non-Fiction

THE NEW SOVIET PSYCHIC DISCOVERIES			
	Henry Gris & William Dick	£1.50	☐
STAR SIGNS FOR LOVERS	Robert Worth	£1.50	☐
THE DAY THE BOMB FELL	Clyde W. Burleson	£1.25	☐
SECRETS OF OUR SPACESHIP MOON	Don Wilson	£1.10	☐

All Sphere books are available at your local bookshop or newsagent, or can be ordered direct from the publisher. Just tick the titles you want and fill in the form below.

Name..

Address...

....

Write to Sphere Books, Cash Sales Department, P.O. Box 11, Falmouth, Cornwall TR10 9EN.

Please enclose cheque or postal order to the value of the cover price plus:

UK: 25p for the first book plus 12p per copy for each additional book ordered to a maximum charge of £1.05.

OVERSEAS: 40p for the first book and 12p for each additional book.

BFPO & EIRE: 25p for the first book plus 10p per copy for the next 8 books, thereafter 5p per book.

Sphere Books reserve the right to show new retail prices on covers which may differ from those previously advertised in the text or elsewhere, and to increase postal rates in accordance with the PO.